GW00792311

Eat, Pray, Share

**'While they were eating, Jesus took bread,
gave thanks and broke it ... saying,
"Take and eat; this is my body."'**
Matthew 26:26

Selwyn Hughes
Revised and updated by Mick Brooks
FURTHER STUDY: IAN SEWTER

© CWR 2012. Dated text previously published as *Every Day
with Jesus: The World's Most Sacred Table* (Mar/Apr 1988) by
CWR. This edition revised and updated for 2013 by Mick Brooks.

CWR, Waverley Abbey House, Waverley Lane, Farnham, Surrey GU9 8EP, UK
Tel: 01252 784700 Email: mail@cwr.org.uk
Registered Charity No. 294387. Registered Limited Company No. 1990308.

Unless otherwise stated, all Scripture quotations are from the Holy Bible,
New International Version. © International Bible Society.

Cover image: Getty/Lina Aidukaite
Quiet Time image: NASA/HST/ASU/J. Hester et al
Printed in England by Linney Print

MIX
Paper from
responsible sources
FSC® C015900
www.fsc.org

Every Day with Jesus is available in **large print** from CWR. It is also available on **audio and DAISY**
in the UK and Eire for the sole use of those with a visual impairment worse than N12, or who are
registered blind. For details please contact **Torch Trust for the Blind**, Tel: 01858 438260.
Torch Trust for the Blind, Torch House, Torch Way, Northampton Road, Market Harborough, LE16 9HL.

A word of introduction ...

I am of the opinion that some of the most significant moments of our lives happen whilst we are sitting at a table. We spend a great deal of time sitting at or around tables: the family breakfast table or dinner table, school tables, work tables, lecture tables and so on.

There is a play called *The Dining Room* in which just a few actors play many different parts. They re-enact all the things that go on around the dining table in the home of an average family: the arguments, the announcements, the emotions and the experiences – including surprise, joy, disappointment, misunderstanding, laughter and countless others! The play ends with just the grandfather and the grandson sitting together at the table, reflecting on these things as the stage lights fade to black and the curtain comes down.

However, for us it will be different. When the curtain of time comes down and the Church is gathered together in eternity, one of the very first things we will see will be a table set for the celebration of the marriage supper of the Lamb. What a day that will be! No more death, sorrow, crying or tears. The great handkerchief of love will be taken out and every tear will be dried.

In this issue Selwyn explores with us the most amazing table of all, a prelude to this great feast to come. I hope that these devotions will change what for some may have become ritual and routine, to become revival and refreshing.

Wishing you a special and blessed Easter

Sincerely yours, in His name

Mick

Mick Brooks, Consulting Editor

 Free small-group resources to accompany this issue can be found at www.cwr.org.uk/extra. The EDWJ Facebook community is growing! To join the conversation visit www.facebook.com/edwjpage

An urgent need

FOR READING & MEDITATION - 1 CORINTHIANS 10:14-22
'... you cannot have a part in both the Lord's table and the table of demons.' (v.21)

Our theme for this Easter season, 'Eat, Pray, Share', is one that I hope will draw us in thought and spirit towards the great sacrifice which Jesus made for us on the cross of Calvary. In this issue we will be considering the Communion table, a central feature of most Christian churches, at which is celebrated the event variously described as 'The Sacrament', 'Holy Communion', 'The Lord's Supper', 'The Lord's Table', 'The Eucharist' or 'The Breaking of Bread'.

Almost every Christian participates from time to time in a service of Communion, but how many of us, I wonder, understand the rich significance that lies behind the simple act of taking and sharing the bread and drinking the wine? Over the years I have inquired of many people of all denominations as to how they understand the act of 'Holy Communion' and, generally speaking, I have discovered only a superficial understanding. Why is it that an event which was intended by Jesus to be a source of continuous spiritual enrichment is, for many, nothing more than a ritual? *I am convinced myself that one of the most urgent needs of the contemporary Christian Church is to return meaning to the Communion.*

FURTHER STUDY

Luke 24:28-35;
1 Cor. 11:23-32

1. When did the disciples recognise Jesus?

2. Why might some be weak?

When we fail to appreciate the meaning of this deeply significant act, then our meeting together around the 'Lord's Table' will have little impact on our lives – individually or corporately. I believe that those who see it as nothing more than a sentimental forget-me-not service will, as a result, be spiritually poorer. Those who see it for what it is – a service of deep spiritual significance – will be continually enriched, enlightened and satisfied.

My Father and my God, help me to see, as I begin these meditations, that whatever table I sit at, none is more sacred and special than Your table. Reveal to me more clearly than ever before its meaning and its purpose. In Christ's name I pray. Amen.

The law of first occurrence

FOR READING & MEDITATION - MATTHEW 26:17-30

'While they were eating, Jesus took bread, gave thanks and broke it, and gave it to his disciples ...' (v.26)

Today we ask ourselves: if the Christian Church is greatly in need of returning meaning to the Communion, where do we start? There is a law of biblical interpretation known as 'the law of first occurrence' which states that whenever you wish to understand a truth of Scripture, you should examine in detail the first occasion when that truth is mentioned.

If we are to understand the deep meaning that lies in the commemorative act of Holy Communion, then our first task must be to focus our attention on the very first Communion service in history – the one conducted by Jesus that famous night in the Upper Room. When a jeweller wants to show off a diamond to its best advantage, he often puts it on a background of black velvet. There, as natural or artificial light strikes it, the diamond catches fire, whereupon its beauty and brilliance is greatly magnified and its value made more apparent.

FURTHER STUDY

Luke 22:39-53

1. Identify Jesus' emotions on that night.

2. How did Jesus shine in the dark?

The Lord's Supper is like that diamond. It needs to be prised from its traditional setting, where, by reason of endless controversy, it borders on becoming lack-lustre, and set against the velvet of the blackest night in history – the night before Jesus was crucified. It is only there, in its original setting, with the light of the Holy Spirit falling upon it, that it yields its true and proper meaning. And I say again – if we do not understand what happened at that very first Communion service, then we will not be able to understand what it means for us now – here in the twenty-first century.

O God, thank You that it is Your Holy Spirit who illuminates the truth. As a diamond catches fire, help me to understand the brilliance of the act of Holy Communion. Amen.

The Christ of the unexpected

FOR READING & MEDITATION - JOHN 2:13-25; 6:1-14

'... at the Passover Feast, many people saw the miraculous signs he was doing and believed in his name.' (John 2:23)

Before we begin a detailed examination of the first Communion service in history (which, as you know, was also Jesus' last collective event with His disciples), we refer briefly to the event that led to the institution of what we now call 'Holy Communion' – namely, the feast of the Passover. More will be said about this later, but the feast of the Passover was the annual celebration of the night when God passed over the land of Egypt and spared the firstborn of the children of Israel. It is still celebrated by many Jews today.

It is probable that Jesus and His disciples had shared together in the ceremony of the Passover on previous occasions, but we cannot be certain. According to John, we know, however, that the disciples had been with Him on two previous Passover festivals, and on both these occasions, something unexpected and unusual had taken place. On the first occasion, Jesus entered the Temple and in an act of righteous indignation, proceeded to empty it of the money changers who, He said, had turned His Father's house into 'a den of robbers' (Luke 19:46). On the second occasion, He performed the miracle of the feeding of the 5,000 (John 6:1-14).

FURTHER STUDY

Deut. 16:1-8;
Luke 2:41-51

1. Why and how was Passover to be celebrated?

2. How did Jesus surprise people at Passover?

I wonder, as once again the Passover approached, did the disciples think to themselves: what surprises will the Master have for us on this occasion? Will He once again do the unexpected and the unusual? It is only conjecture, of course, but if this thought did arise in their minds, they could have had no idea that they were about to be witnesses at the most central Passover of all time, and be observers of an event that would change the entire course of history.

O Father, help me never to forget that You are the God of the unusual and the unexpected. Show me that when I follow You and Your Son, there are surprises around every corner. Thank You, dear Father. Amen.

Believing the Master's word

FOR READING & MEDITATION - LUKE 22:7-13
'They left and found things just as Jesus had told them.' (v.13)

If, as we said yesterday, the disciples were wondering whether Jesus might once again perform the unusual and unexpected at the Passover feast, we can see from our passage today that they were not left wondering for long. At the beginning of the Passover, the Master issues them with a set of very unusual and unexpected instructions. 'Go into the city', He tells them, 'and you will see a man carrying a pitcher of water; follow him and he will take you to a room where we will celebrate the Passover together.'

FURTHER STUDY

John 2:1-11;
Heb. 11:8-10,
17-19

1. What was the result of obeying Jesus?

2. How are faith and obedience related?

There can be little doubt that the knowledge Jesus had concerning the man and the room was supernatural, but there is another point to be noted here: that is, the complete and utter confidence the disciples had in the word and command of Jesus. No one remonstrated with Him and said, 'But, Master, men don't usually carry pitchers of water – that is normally a task that women perform.' Neither did they say, 'Lord, what will this man think of us when we attempt to follow him?' The disciples had obviously learned to trust the word of Jesus and to act without questioning His commands.

That is a lesson every one of us sorely needs to learn. How often things go wrong in our lives because we quibble over Jesus' words. I wonder, am I talking to someone at this very moment who is hesitating or drawing back from something the Master has shown you that He wants you to do? If so, then let me give you the word that Mary, Jesus' mother, once gave to a group of interested but hesitant people: 'Do whatever he tells you' (John 2:5).

O Father, how expertly You put Your finger on my need. I am often afraid to do what You ask me to do – afraid that it might not be in my best interests or that I might make a fool of myself. Help me see how foolish that is. Amen.

CWR Ministry Events
PLEASE PRAY FOR THE TEAM

DATE	EVENT	PLACE	PRESENTER(S)
1–3 Mar	Preparation for Marriage	Waverley Abbey House	Mick & Lynette Brooks with Andrew & Lynn Penson
2 Mar	Small Group Leaders' Toolbox	WAH	Andy Peck
8 Mar	God Unannounced	WAH	Andy Peck
11–15 Mar	Pastoral Care in the Local Church	WAH	Stuart Pascall, Lynn Penson and Team
18–22 Mar	Introduction to Biblical Care and Counselling	WAH	Angie Coombes and Team
21 Mar	Insight Day: Helping Couples with Troubled Marriages	Pilgrim Hall	Heather & Ian Churchill
25 Mar	Passover Supper	PH	Elizabeth Hodkinson
26 Mar	Passover Supper	WAH	Elizabeth Hodkinson
4 Apr	Leading a Church in a Driven World	WAH	Andy Peck
6 Apr	Successfully Navigating the Teenage Years	WAH	Owen & Laura Ashley
9 Apr	Transformational Leadership	WAH	Coleen Jackson and Robin Precey
19 Apr	Counselling Enquirers' Event	PH	Counselling Team
24 Apr	Managing Conflict Creatively	WAH	Chris Ledger
25 Apr	The Bible in a Day	WAH	Andy Peck
26–28 Apr	Women's Weekend: 'Springs of Life'	WAH	Nicky-Sue Terry and Ros Derges
2 May	Small Group Leaders' Evening	WAH	Andy Peck
7–9 May	Bible Discovery Weekend: 'The Pebble Who Became a Rock'	PH	Philip Greenslade
11 May	Understanding Yourself, Understanding Others (MBTI® Basic)	WAH	Andrew & Lynn Penson
28 May – 1 Jun	The Big Story	WAH	Philip Greenslade

Please also pray for students and tutors on our ongoing **BA in Counselling** programme at Waverley and Pilgrim Hall and our **Certificate and Diploma of Christian Counselling** and **MA in Integrative Psychotherapy** held at London School of Theology.

For further details and a full list of CWR's courses, phone +44 (0)1252 784719 or visit the CWR website at www.cwr.org.uk

The 'Pass-over'

FOR READING & MEDITATION – EXODUS 12:1-13

'The blood will be a sign for you ... and when I see the blood,
I will pass over you.' (v.13)

If we are to comprehend the real meaning of the Communion, then we must begin to understand what the feast of the Passover was all about, for it was out of that that the first Communion service emerged. During the time of Israel's bondage and slavery in Egypt, God spoke to Pharaoh through Moses and warned him that on a certain day, at the hour of midnight, He was going to pass through the land and strike down every firstborn. There was to be no discrimination between human beings and animals, or between different social classes – every firstborn would die.

FURTHER STUDY

Lev. 4:27-35;
17:11;
1 Pet. 1:18-21

1. What is special about blood?

2. What is special about Christ's blood?

God then devised a plan whereby the firstborn of His own people, the Israelites, would be protected. Each Israelite was to choose a lamb (a year-old male without defect) and kill it. They were then to take some of the lamb's blood, dip a branch of hyssop in it and sprinkle it on the lintel and side posts of their front door. They were not to go out of the house at all that night. Having shed and sprinkled the blood, they must shelter under it. At midnight God passed through the land, and in every house which did not have a blood-sprinkled door, the firstborn died. The God who passed *through* Egypt in judgment passed *over* every blood-marked dwelling place – hence the term, 'Pass-over'.

It is worth noting – if rubies or some other precious stones had gleamed like red flames from every door, it would not have saved the firstborn of the children of Israel. God had decreed that it was only by the shedding of blood that they were to be saved. If the Israelites had stumbled here, they would never have made it to this point in history.

My Father, I realise that this question of redemption by blood is of vital importance, even for us today. Help me to grasp the immensity of the sacrifice Jesus made in shedding His blood that I might be redeemed. For His name's sake. Amen.

'This is a day you are to commemorate; for the generations to come ... celebrate it as a festival to the LORD ...' (v.14)

As an understanding of the feast of the Passover is a vital key to comprehending the meaning that lies behind the act of 'Holy Communion', we must spend another day exploring it further. On Passover night itself, the Israelites were bidden to feast on a roasted lamb, with bitter herbs and unleavened bread, and they were to do so with their cloak tucked into their belt, their sandals on their feet and their staff in their hand, ready to make a quick departure from the land of slavery.

The night of the Passover was so important that it marked the beginning of a new year for Israel – 'This month is to be ... the first month of your year' (12:2). From that day to this, the Jewish religious new year begins with *Pesach* – the Hebrew word for 'Passover'. God gave the Israelites an instruction that this feast should be commemorated throughout the generations to come, and families should explain to their children what the whole ceremony meant: 'It is the Passover sacrifice to the LORD, who passed over the houses of the Israelites in Egypt and spared our homes when he struck the Egyptians' (v.27).

This celebration was to last seven days and was known as the Feast of Unleavened Bread, during which time the Israelites were to remind themselves that their deliverance from Egypt's bondage had been planned by Jehovah, purchased by blood and implemented by divine power. Being a redeemed people, this meant that they belonged to the Almighty in a special way and were therefore to be consecrated to His service and be an illustration to the world of what redeemed people should be like.

FURTHER STUDY

Exod. 13:1-16;
2 Chron. 30:21-27

1. How was Passover to be a 'passing on'?

2. How did the Israelites experience a double blessing?

Father, the implications of all this go deep into my soul as I reflect on whether I am an illustration to the world of what a redeemed person should be like. I take a step closer to You today. Make me what I ought to be. In Jesus' name. Amen.

The Passover table

FOR READING & MEDITATION – MARK 14:12-16
'So they prepared the Passover.' (v.16)

Having seen what the feast of the Passover means and why it was to be celebrated annually, we return now to the details of the last Passover feast which Jesus commemorated with His disciples. Upon finding the room in which the Master purposed to celebrate the Passover, the disciples began at once to make the preparations for the feast.

Although every one of the four Gospels contains an account of the Last Supper, we are not given any details as to how the feast was prepared and what items were placed on the Passover table. We know from the instructions given by God in the Old Testament and tradition that certain items would be laid out on the table. There would have been a supply of bitter herbs – a reminder of the suffering that their forefathers went through in Egypt. Another item would have been a bowl of salt water to remind them of the tears that were shed during the years of bondage and slavery. A further item would have been grated apple mixed with nuts and made into a paste (called *charoseth*) which would resemble the colour of clay and thus remind them of the endless amount of bricks that were made in Egypt.

FURTHER STUDY

2 Chron. 35:1-19;
1 Cor. 5:6-8

1. What was special about Josiah?

2. How is Christ linked to Passover?

Yet another item would have been unleavened bread, the absence of yeast symbolising the haste of that unforgettable night and also the need to break with the leaven of evil. On the table, too, would have been an egg symbolising new life, candles to remind them of the worship that went on in the tabernacle, wine to symbolise the shedding of blood, and last but not least – a roasted lamb. All this had a supreme and important purpose – the event must be kept alive in the memory of Israel. For great events ought never to be forgotten.

Lord Jesus, help me see the value of keeping alive in my memory the great Passover act that You accomplished for me on Calvary. May the wonder of it reverberate within my being yet again this day. In Your dear name I ask it. Amen.

FOR READING & MEDITATION - PSALM 19:7-14

'The law of the Lord is perfect, reviving the soul. The statutes of the Lord are trustworthy ...' (v.7)

Before looking in detail at the Passover which Jesus shared with His disciples, we must pause to deal with a relevant but sometimes controversial issue. I refer to the fact that at first glance, there appears to be a contradiction in Scripture as to the actual date of that Passover. The difficulty can be seen when we compare two separate passages of Scripture, the first in Luke 22:15 and the second in John 18:28. The first reads, 'And he said to them, "I have eagerly desired to eat this Passover with you before I suffer"'. The second says, 'Then the Jews led Jesus from Caiaphas to the palace of the Roman governor. By now it was early morning, and to avoid ceremonial uncleanness the Jews did not enter the palace; they wanted to be able to eat the Passover.'

The first passage shows Jesus eating the Passover with His disciples on Thursday, while the second shows the priests, early the next morning, refusing to go into the palace because the Passover had not yet been celebrated. Does that mean (as many have supposed) that what Jesus celebrated with His disciples was not the Passover but a simple family meal? No, for Jesus says, quite clearly, 'I have eagerly desired to eat *this* Passover with you ...'

Tomorrow we will explore further these two passages, but it is important to keep in mind that God's Word is without contradiction. Some passages of the Bible may look, at first glance, to be contradictory, but we must remember that we may not have the key that reconciles the two apparently contradictory passages. The inspired Scriptures can be relied on, and we can ask God to help us gain deeper understanding.

FURTHER STUDY

Psa. 119:97-104;
2 Tim. 3:14-17;
2 Pet. 1:16-21

1. What was the psalmist's testimony?

2. What is the origin of Scripture?

Gracious and loving heavenly Father, help me to have confidence in Your Word, for I know that You are trustworthy. Give me a heart that longs to know more of Your truth, and guide me as I explore further. Amen.

A suggested reconciliation

FOR READING & MEDITATION - 1 CORINTHIANS 5:1-8

'For Christ, our Passover lamb, has been sacrificed.' (v.7)

We continue looking at the two apparently contradictory passages which we brought up in our discussion yesterday. There have been many attempts to harmonise these passages, one view being that Jesus, anticipating the fact that He would die on the night the Passover would be celebrated (Friday) decided to celebrate it one day earlier with His disciples. Another view says that as John's statement contradicts the other three Gospel writers, he was obviously mistaken in what he wrote. Those who believe in the inspiration of Scripture (as I do) find these explanations unacceptable.

FURTHER STUDY

Isa. 53:1-12;
John 1:29-34

1. Why is Jesus likened to a lamb?

2. Why did Jesus endure suffering?

The best reconciliation I have read is that offered by Joachim Jeremias in his book, *The Eucharistic Words of Jesus*, in which he says that it was possible for the Passover to be eaten *officially* on two nights of the year. He claims that during this period of history, the Pharisees and Sadducees were using calendars which differed from each other by a day. One group celebrated it a day earlier than the other, and in the light of this, it was possible for Jesus to eat the Passover with those who followed the Pharisees (Thursday) and go to the cross on Friday at the time that the other group were beginning their Passover celebrations.

If this was so, then it adds a rich and wondrous meaning to the words of our text today: 'For Christ, our Passover lamb, has been sacrificed.' It would mean that Jesus actually died on the cross at the very time the ritualistic lambs were being slaughtered by the Sadducees at the Temple in Jerusalem.

O Father, help me to see that for every contradiction, there is a reconciliation. Teach me how to look for this reconciliation, not only in Your Word but in the seeming contradictions of my daily life. For Jesus' sake. Amen.

The seed of faith, with love ...

... from you, to Christians in need, both at home and overseas, who seek – like you – the guidance to live their everyday lives as God wills.

Jesus said, 'The kingdom of heaven is like a mustard seed, which a man took and planted in his field. Though it is the smallest of all your seeds, yet when it grows it ... becomes a tree, so that the birds of the air come and perch in its branches' (Matt. 13:31-32).

Please help CWR to root deeply people's beliefs.

Please fill in the 'Gift to CWR' section on the order form at the back of this publication, completing the Gift Aid declaration if appropriate.

Great enough to be humble

FOR READING & MEDITATION - JOHN 13:1-17

'... he poured water into a basin and began to wash
his disciples' feet ...' (v.5)

We move on now to focus our attention on the interesting
and dramatic events that went on in the Upper Room
in Jerusalem where Jesus observed the Passover feast with
His disciples. Picture the scene with me. It is dusk, and
Jesus and His disciples are reclining around a low table in
an atmosphere that is heavy with unborn events. Outside
a storm is brewing that will eventually engulf the Son of
God and sweep Him towards the cross. Jesus had already
seen the sun set for the last time. In less than 18 hours, His
limbs would be stretched on what one writer calls those
'grisly timbers of torture'; within 24 hours, He
would be dead.

**FURTHER
STUDY**

Mark 10:35-45;
Phil. 2:1-11

1. Contrast
Jesus and the
disciples.

2. How can
we show the
same attitude
as Jesus?

Evidently no servant was in attendance to wash
the feet of those present – a usual courtesy of the
day – so Jesus rises from the table, strips off His
outer clothing and, taking a towel and a bowl of
water, proceeds to wash the disciples' feet. We
said earlier that the disciples would face many
surprises at this last crucial Passover. This was
another – in the form of the Saviour who stooped
to wash their feet.

Isn't it interesting that *none* of the disciples
volunteered for that lowly task? They were so
unsure of themselves that they dared not be humble – such
an action might have caused them to lose their frail sense
of identity. Jesus, on the other hand, had such a clear sense
of identity – knowing that He had come from God and was
going to God – that He could choose to be humble. How sad
that the disciples were willing to fight over a throne, but
not over a towel. Things don't seem to have changed much
in 21 centuries, do they?

**Gracious and loving Father, forgive me that I too am more
interested in a throne than a towel; more concerned about
status than I am about serving. O Father, help me become more
like Jesus. For His own dear name's sake. Amen.**

Humility – a choice

MON
11 MAR

FOR READING & MEDITATION – MATTHEW 20:17-28

'... the Son of Man did not come to be served, but to serve,
and to give his life as a ransom for many.' (v.28)

We said yesterday that Jesus was so conscious of greatness that He could afford to be humble. What does this really mean? Consider once again the account given by the apostle John: 'Jesus knew that the Father had put all things under his power, and that he had come from God and was returning to God; so he got up from the meal, took off his outer clothing, and wrapped a towel round his waist ... he poured water into a basin and began to wash his disciples' feet' (John 13:3–5).

Notice how John, under the inspiration of the Holy Spirit, sees right into the mind of Jesus before He stoops down to wash the disciples' feet. And what does he see? He sees Jesus' consciousness of His own greatness – 'Jesus knew ... that he had come from God and was returning to God ...'

The consciousness of greatness is the secret of humility. Those who do not have a high sense of their worth and value in God can never, in the true sense of the word, be humble. Their 'humility' borders more on self-belittlement. They do not *choose* to be humble, for more often than not, they are forced into situations which they can do very little about except say to themselves, 'Well, now that I am here, I will be humble.'

Humility is always a choice – a choice which arises out of a high sense of one's worth and value. Look at this phrase: 'Jesus knew that the Father had put all things under his power ...' Everything was under His power! And what did He do with that power? He used it to take a towel, pour water into a bowl and wash the disciples' feet. Knowing who He was made Him great – and humble. Great because humble, and humble because great.

FURTHER STUDY

Luke 22:24-30;
Gal. 5:13-14

1. How did Jesus describe His role?

2. Why should we serve others?

O Father, if it is true that the consciousness of greatness is the secret of humility, then give me a vision today, not only of Your greatness, but of my greatness also – my greatness in You. In Christ's name I pray. Amen.

'No, not my feet!'

FOR READING & MEDITATION - 1 PETER 5:1-11

'Clothe (apron) yourselves, all of you, with humility
[as the garb of a servant ...]' (v.5, Amplified Bible)

We spend another day looking at that moving moment when Jesus began washing the disciples' feet. I can imagine that by the time Jesus got to Simon Peter, the arguing and small talk that had been going on among the disciples would have diminished. No doubt they began to realise how slow and insensitive they had been not to take the servant's role themselves. But as Jesus bends before Peter, the disciple almost shouts, 'No! Not my feet! You shall never wash my feet.'

Is that what humility is – refusing to let Jesus wash one's feet? Of course not. In fact, it sometimes takes more humility to be ministered to than it does to minister. You see, when we are always giving out to others, it is fairly easy to cover up our pride, but when we are put on the receiving end and others are ministering to us, then our pride has nowhere to hide. Jesus said some strong words to Peter at this point: 'Unless I wash you, you have no part with me.' This firm statement penetrated Peter's defences, but rather than face his pride, he found another way out – the way of over-reaction: 'Then, Lord ... not just my feet but my hands and my head as well!'

FURTHER STUDY

Col. 3:22-24;
1 John 3:16-18

1. How should we serve others?

2. What is true love?

After Jesus had brought about some balance in Peter's life and had finished washing the disciples' feet, He sat back at the table and gave them this instruction, 'Now that I, your Lord and Teacher, have washed your feet, you also should wash one another's feet.' Notice the words – 'one another's feet'. Had He said, 'You should wash my feet', every disciple would have clamoured for the privilege. Who wouldn't stand in line to wash the Saviour's feet? But 'one another's feet' – ah, that's different. That puts obedience to its maximum test.

Lord Jesus Christ, You who stooped to wash the disciples' feet, put in my heart this very day that same spirit of humility and love. Make of me what You can, dear Lord. For Your own dear name's sake. Amen.

Judas the betrayer

FOR READING & MEDITATION - JOHN 13:18-30

'As soon as Judas had taken the bread, he went out.
And it was night.' (v.30)

We look now at another scene from the great drama that was enacted in the Upper Room on that first Maundy Thursday – Jesus' confrontation with Judas. It must have come as a great surprise to Judas when the Master made the announcement that there was someone present who was about to betray Him. E.F. Kevan says, 'It was the custom at the Passover feast for the presiding father, if there was an especially honoured guest, to break off a large piece of bread and give it to him first. It was that large piece that Jesus gave to Judas.'

As soon as Judas received the bread from Jesus' hand, we read that 'Satan entered into him'. He then went out to put into action his plan of betrayal and the Scripture cryptically says, 'And it was night.' Night in Jerusalem, and night in his soul! How it must have hurt Jesus to have been betrayed by one of His own disciples. In this hard and cruel world, people expect to be shot at by their enemies, but no one, except a cynic, expects to be shot at by his friends.

Did you know that the origin of the superstition concerning the number thirteen stems from this scene in the Gospels? Thirteen sat down at the Last Supper, and one of them was a traitor. Superstitious people have dreaded the number thirteen ever since. Have you ever been betrayed? It's not easy to remain unembittered when someone who has stood at your side and claimed to be your friend lets you down. Jesus, despite the pain that the knowledge of Judas' betrayal caused Him, did not allow it to deter Him from ministering to the other disciples. Nor, too, must we.

FURTHER STUDY

Psa. 41:1-13;
Heb. 12:14-15

1. Identify the psalmist's emotions.

2. How can we remain unembittered?

Lord Jesus, I am thankful that You make it possible for me to go on even when I am in pain. And whenever I am next let down, help me to drink deeply of Your own determination – and keep on ministering to others. For Your name's sake. Amen.

Accountant turned embezzler

FOR READING & MEDITATION - 1 TIMOTHY 6:3-19

'For the love of money is a root of all kinds of evil.' (v.10)

Today we ask ourselves: who was Judas Iscariot and how do we explain his involvement in the betrayal of Jesus? It is believed by most Bible commentators that Judas was a Judean, and if this was true, then he would have been the only member of the apostolic band who was a southerner. Observe that, for it is not unimportant. Eleven of Christ's disciples were Galileans and only one came from the south. This would have meant that not only did Judas speak with a different accent, but also his views and outlook on things would have been quite different from the rest of the group.

FURTHER STUDY

Matt. 6:19-34;
John 12:1-6

1. How can money be our master?

2. Describe Judas's character.

This might have put him a little bit on his own from the start. I am saying this, I hasten to add, not to excuse him, but to explain him.

It seems also that he was a man with a commercial mind, for he was appointed to be the treasurer of the party – the 'keeper of the money bag' (John 12:6). The little company, as it moved from place to place, needed someone to handle simple purchases, and as Judas possessed some business acumen, he was the one chosen for the task. But Judas was not just a man with a business mind: he was also a man with a covetous heart. We are told that he had been dipping into the money bag for a long time before he took the traitorous step of betraying Jesus.

With some natures, there is nothing so holy that money cannot besmirch it. Watch money – it is so terribly useful and yet so terribly dangerous. What is dangerous is not the money itself, but the way in which it can tempt us to become attached to it. When money becomes our god, then a susceptible personality is the price we pay for the worship of that god.

Gracious and loving heavenly Father, show me how to cut out of my nature that 'root of all evil' – the love of money. I want money to be my servant, not my master. Help me, dear Lord, in this quest. For Jesus' sake I pray. Amen.

A free agent

FOR READING & MEDITATION - PSALM 41:1-13

'Even my close friend, whom I trusted ... has lifted up his heel against me.' (v.9)

We spend one more day discussing Judas and his involvement in the betrayal of Jesus. Some Christian writers have expressed great sympathy for Judas. They feel he had an unfair deal in his life and has suffered from a bad press ever since. 'After all,' they say, 'if Jesus had to die, somebody had to betray Him. So why blame Judas? He was but the tool of providence, the victim of predestination.'

The Bible certainly indicates that Jesus foreknew that He would be betrayed by him (see John 6:64), but foreknowledge is not the same thing as foreordination. I know the sun will rise tomorrow, but my knowing it does not make it rise. The foreknowledge that Jesus had concerning Judas did not compel him to act the way he did – he was a free agent in it all. Judas got involved in the act of betrayal by following the same method that every one of us follows when we commit sin – first we are tempted, then, instead of showing it the door, we bring it into our living room and entertain it. After that, the temptation is more difficult to resist and then it is just a step downward into sin.

FURTHER STUDY

1 Cor. 10:1-13;
James 1:12-15

1. What is our consolation when tempted?

2. Outline the process of temptation?

However strong the various influences were around Judas, there must have been a time when he opened himself to them. Jesus clearly regarded him as a responsible agent, for even at the last minute in the Upper Room, He carefully worded His statement so that Judas had an opportunity to recant. So underhand was this action of Judas that throughout history, whenever Maundy Thursday comes around, the first thing that comes into our mind is this – it was the night on which our Saviour was betrayed.

Father, I ask one thing, not that I shall be preserved from being betrayed, but that I shall be preserved from betraying others. And above all – from betraying You. Make me a person who is not only trusting, but trustworthy. In Jesus' name. Amen.

The order of service

FOR READING & MEDITATION - EXODUS 13:1-10

'You must keep this ordinance at the appointed time year
after year.' (v.10)

We turn now from looking at some of the personalities
who were present in the Upper Room when Jesus
conducted the first Communion service to focus on the
Master Himself. I wonder how Jesus felt as He realised that
He was setting up His own memorial service? What were
the things He emphasised as He celebrated this Passover
of all Passovers? Where was the transition point when the
Passover feast took on the nature of a new commemorative
act? These are some of the questions we will come to grips
with over the days that lead up to Good Friday – but first
let's reflect together on the way in which the
Passover meal was conducted.

**FURTHER
STUDY**

Lev. 8:1-12;
2 Thess. 2:13-17

1. How were
the priests
consecrated
or sanctified?

2. How are we
sanctified?

None of the four Gospel writers give exact
and detailed accounts of the traditions that they
followed during a Passover meal – they focused
more on the highlights of that memorable evening
– so we have to depend on sources outside of
Scripture for information concerning this. I am
drawing therefore on the writings of Jewish authors
and the practice of many Jews today, as I describe
to you the tradition of a Passover celebration.

Just after dusk on the night of the Passover, a
Jewish family gather around a table on which has been
laid out the various items I described for you a few days
ago. The meal begins with the father holding up the first
of the four cups that are on the table and praying over it,
then all drink from it. This is called the 'Cup of Kiddush',
meaning separation or sanctification. It was the cup that
separated this meal from all other meals and marked it out
as being different.

**Loving Father, as I come to study the order in which the
Passover feast is conducted, help me to see the ways in which
it conceals Your great plan of eternal salvation. In Jesus' name
I pray. Amen.**

On 25 and 26 March CWR will be holding Passover Suppers. Visit our website for details: www.cwr.org.uk

FOR READING & MEDITATION - EXODUS 6:1-13

'... I have heard the groaning of the Israelites ...
and I have remembered my covenant.' (v.5)

We continue looking at the manner in which the Passover meal was conducted during the time of Christ, and is still conducted by Jews today. We said yesterday that the meal commenced with the drinking of the first of four cups – the 'Cup of Kiddush'. The four cups were reminders of the four promises of Exodus 6:6–7: (1) I will bring you out from under the yoke of the Egyptians; (2) I will free you from being slaves to them; (3) I will redeem you with an outstretched arm and with mighty acts of judgment; (4) I will take you as my own people, and I will be your God.

After the drinking of the first cup, the host would take a bowl of water and a towel and pass them around the table so that all could wash their hands. He would then draw attention to the bitter herbs and the bowl of salt water that were on the table, which they would all be invited to taste – a reminder of the bitterness of slavery in Egypt and of the tears that had been shed so profusely by their forefathers.

Then the main course would be brought out, which consists of roast lamb, although it would not be eaten yet. The family would be reminded that it was through the shed blood of a lamb that their homes had been protected when the destroyer passed through Egypt. Their attention would be drawn, too, to the presence of the unleavened bread on the table and how they had to leave behind them all reminders of the culture when fleeing from Egypt, including the leaven for their bread. Then would come the second eating of bitter herbs, a further reminder of the bitterness of slavery. A further benediction was then offered in gratitude to God for His deliverance on that dark and fateful night.

FURTHER STUDY

Matt. 6:1-5;
Luke 12:1;
1 Cor. 5:6-8

1. What was the yeast or leaven of the Pharisees?

2. What are we to leave behind?

O God, I sense that wondrous and miraculous though that first Passover night was, it was but a dress rehearsal for another and greater Passover - the deliverance wrought through our Lord's sacrifice on the cross. I am eternally grateful. Amen.

The eating of the lamb

FOR READING & MEDITATION - EXODUS 15:1-19

'By the power of your arm they will be as still as a stone
- until your people pass by, O LORD ...' (v.16)

We continue looking at the way in which the Passover meal was celebrated, as it is an important and necessary background to our understanding of the Lord's Supper. After the second eating of the bitter herbs would come the drinking of the second cup, which was called the 'Cup of Haggadah' or the 'Cup of Explanation'. The father would once again lead the family in the drinking of this cup.

At this point, the youngest son in the family would be prompted formally to ask a series of questions starting with, 'Why is this night different from all other nights?' The head of the household would then give a potted history of Israel right down to the deliverance of the Passover, explaining how this demonstrated God's everlasting power and mercy. Following this would begin the singing of the first part of what was called the Egyptian Hallel – the name given to the group of psalms of praise from Psalm 113 to Psalm 118, which were used for Passover. Designated here were just Psalms 113 and 114.

Next came a second act of hand washing. The host would wash his hands and then prepare a 'sop' – a piece of unleavened bread filled with lamb and dipped in the paste called the *charoseth*. He would give the sop to the honoured guest on his left, then to others sitting around the table. It was this 'sop' Jesus offered to Judas (in place of the honoured guest) who, at this point in the Last Supper, left to betray Him (John 13:26–30). Following this would come the eating of the meal, the roasted lamb, which by tradition had to be wholly eaten. Anything left over was to be destroyed and not used for a common meal.

FURTHER STUDY

Psa. 114:1-8;
James 4:1-8

1. Why would the first part of the Hallel be relevant?

2. What should we do as well as wash our hands?

Loving Father, as I follow these procedures, I see how painstaking You were in preparing Your people for that Passover of all Passovers. Understanding each part will help me gain more from each Lord's Supper I celebrate. Thank You. Amen.

'The Hallel'

'Give thanks to the LORD, for he is good. *His love endures for ever.*'

(v.1)

We spend one more day exploring the formalities of the Passover meal. Once the lamb had been eaten, then came the drinking of the third cup – called the 'Cup of Thanksgiving'. This cup was served with a piece of unleavened bread. Once the cup had been drunk, the host would then give thanks for the meal that they had eaten, after which would follow the singing of the rest of the Egyptian Hallel – Psalms 115 to 118. Then the fourth cup would be drunk, whereupon the family would sing what is known as 'The Hallel' – the psalm before us today. The singing of 'The Hallel' would bring the Passover meal to its conclusion.

FURTHER STUDY

Psa. 118:1-29;
Acts 4:10-12

1. How might Psalm 118 relate to Jesus?

2. What did Peter explain?

We cannot be certain, of course, whether or not Jesus followed this precise pattern at the Passover feast He celebrated with His disciples, although I think we can safely assume that apart from those moments when He gave the Passover a new direction, He did. It's interesting to note that none of the Gospels go into detail about the exact location of the room, the position of the disciples around our Lord, or the number of artefacts upon the table – all these things seemed to be considered as relatively unimportant.

What was important – and every Gospel writer recorded it – was the stunning revelation that Jesus gave concerning a new commemorative act that would become the ultimate Passover feast. No wonder Jesus said, at the beginning of the meal, 'I have eagerly desired to eat this Passover with you before I suffer' (Luke 22:15). He longed to let them know that the story of His death had been hidden all the time within the Passover celebration – waiting to be revealed.

Blessed Lord Jesus, I bow in adoration and worship before You as I contemplate the eagerness with which You reached out to the cross. 'All this Thou didst for me – what can I now do for Thee?' Amen.

Born to die

FOR READING & MEDITATION – JOHN 12:20-36

'No, it was for this very reason I came to this hour.' (v.27)

Now that we have familiarised ourselves with the traditional manner in which the feast of the Passover was conducted, we ask ourselves: what must have been going on in the heart and mind of the Master as He shared the Passover meal with His disciples? He was clearly aware of the fact that His death was imminent, for, as we saw yesterday, He had said, 'I have eagerly desired to eat this Passover with you before I suffer.'

The astonishing thing is that even though our Lord knew that within 24 hours He would be dead and buried, it was clear that He was thinking of His mission, not as something that was past, but as something that yet awaited Him. Normally, a person who has lived barely half the allotted span of life, when told that he is about to die, is plunged into deep depression. Kübler-Ross, the famous anthropologist, who made a special study of the reactions people go through when they know they are about to die, said that there are five clear stages through which a person passes when confronted by the news that death is imminent.

FURTHER STUDY

John 18:36-37;
1 Tim. 1:12-17

1. What was Christ's great purpose?

2. How can Christ's purpose become ours?

I watched my wife go through these five stages when her doctors informed her that her sickness was terminal. But I find nothing of this in the heart and mind of Jesus. He suffered intense grief in the Garden of Gethsemane but, as we shall see, this was not because He was unprepared or unwilling to die. The cross was not something our Lord ever tried to avoid: it was the reason why He came. He saw the cross, not as the end of His mission, but as the accomplishment of it – His lifelong goal.

Blessed Lamb of God, slain from the foundation of the world, give me an ever-increasing consciousness of the love that led You to leave the eternal throne and die on the cross for me. I am so deeply, deeply thankful. Amen.

For insight on the subject of bereavement, see CWR's *The Path Not Chosen* by Wendy Bray. www.cwr.org.uk

Startling vehemence

FOR READING & MEDITATION – MATTHEW 16:21-28

'... Jesus began to explain to his disciples that he must go to Jerusalem and suffer many things ...' (v.21)

We said yesterday that Christ's death was not something He wanted to avoid: indeed it was the very reason why He came into the world. He was born to die.

Do you know that great painting by Holman Hunt entitled 'The Shadow of Death'? It depicts the inside of the carpenter's shop in Nazareth and shows Jesus, stripped to the waist, standing by a wooden trestle on which He has put down His awl. He is obviously a little tired and stretches both His arms towards heaven. As He does so, the evening sunlight, flooding in through the open door of the little carpenter's shop, casts a dark shadow in the form of a cross on the wall behind Him. In the foreground can be seen His mother, Mary, who, kneeling among the chips of wood, looks up and is obviously startled as she sees her Son's cross-like shadow on the wall.

Some regard this painting as sickly and sentimental, but the idea it contains is a scriptural one – the cross loomed large in the mind and perspective of Jesus, probably from His earliest days and certainly from the commencement of His ministry. The verse before us today is the first prediction of His passion. There had been passing allusions to it before, but here it is quite clear that Jesus knew He was destined for a cross. And so horrified was He by Peter's insistence that He put the thought away from Him that He addressed him with strange and uncharacteristic words, 'Out of my way, Satan!' (v.23, J.B. Phillips). The vehemence was not aimed at Peter, but at the satanic ploy that was sounding through him. Nothing could deter Jesus from going to the cross – for He knew that this was the very reason why He had come.

FURTHER STUDY

Matt. 20:17-19; 26:1-2; Luke 24:1-8

1. Why did Jesus speak so much of His death?

2. What was the message of the angels?

My Lord and Saviour, I am grateful beyond words that You allowed nothing to deter You from going to Calvary. Help me show the same determination in the face of a lesser cross that may confront me. For Your own dear name's sake. Amen.

The moment of revelation

FOR READING & MEDITATION - MATTHEW 26:26-30

'This is my blood of the covenant, which is poured out for many for the forgiveness of sins.' (v.28)

We come now to the question which has intrigued Christians in every century of the Christian Church: at what point in the evening did Jesus make clear to His disciples that He was instituting His own commemorative meal? We cannot be absolutely sure, but most commentators believe it was probably after the drinking of the third cup – 'The Cup of Thanksgiving'.

There are two reasons for this belief – one is that Paul, in his letter to the Corinthians, refers to the Communion cup as 'the cup of thanksgiving' (I Cor. 10:16). The second is the fact that 'The Cup of Blessing' was served with a piece of unleavened bread, at which time the head of the household would say, 'This is the bread of affliction which our fathers had to eat as they came out of Egypt.' If this was the moment of revelation, then you can imagine how astonished the disciples must have been when Jesus said those tremendous and powerful words, 'This is my body given for you; do this in remembrance of me', and 'This cup is the new covenant in my blood, which is poured out for you' (Luke 22:19–20).

FURTHER STUDY

John 6:48-59;
1 Cor. 11:23-26

1. How do we feed on Jesus?

2. What part of Passover should we pass on?

This is the impact of what He was saying – 'Never again need you keep as the central focus of your worship the memory of your forefathers' deliverance from Egypt, for I am about to go to my death as the true Passover sacrifice. From now on, I want you to remember regularly an even greater event – the giving of my own body and blood for your redemption.' In a few simple but powerful words, our Lord transformed an ancient ritual into the world's most wondrous revelation.

Lord Jesus, as You interpreted the real meaning of the Passover to those around You that day, help me to interpret the meaning of Your cross to those around me today. Amen.

God's Paschal Lamb

FOR READING & MEDITATION – ISAIAH 53:1-12

'... he was led like a lamb to the slaughter ...' (v.7)

We continue drinking in the wonder of that moment when Jesus revealed to His disciples that He was God's Paschal Lamb, His ultimate sacrificial lamb. In a play, a character standing in the wings with the lighting behind him will cast a long shadow across the stage and, by reason of this, will attract the audience's attention. But when the character himself steps on to the stage, whatever degree of interest the shadow aroused is surpassed by the wonder of seeing the character appear personally.

For centuries, Jesus stood in the wings of history, casting His shadow before Him. He can be seen on almost every page of the Old Testament – in the deliverance of Israel from Egypt, in the sacrifices, in the details of the tabernacle, in the ministry of the priesthood, and so on. Throughout the prophetic books, predictions concerning the coming Messiah give the shadow more detail. Finally, 400 years after the Old Testament times, John the Baptist made the declaration, 'Look, the Lamb of God, who takes away the sin of the world!' (John 1:29). At last, the shadow had substance.

FURTHER STUDY

Rev. 5:1-14; 7:9-10

1. How does Jesus appear in heaven?

2. Why is He praised?

Notice the words, 'the Lamb of God who takes away the *sin of the world*' (my emphasis). The Old Testament shows a progressive revelation as related to the offering of a lamb: first a lamb atoned for an individual, as in the case of Isaac; then for a family, as at the first Passover; then for a nation, as on the Day of Atonement. The world waited for the day when a lamb would come whose sacrifice would take away, not just the sins of an individual, a family or even a nation, but the sins of the entire world. Now that day had arrived. And the sacrifice? None other than Jesus – God's Paschal Lamb.

Gracious Father, I am so thankful that before ever there was a man, there was a lamb. For Jesus, Your Son, is the Lamb who was slain from the foundation of the world. I am eternally grateful. Amen.

God's Story

Getting to grips with the Bible: where to start? CWR tutor Andy Peck introduces *Bible60*, a new resource giving you an overview of the whole Bible narrative in just 60 days.

Over the last few years, many of you have taken up CWR's challenge to read through the entire Bible in a year using our chronological Bible-reading plan, *Cover to Cover Complete*. To many, however, the thought of embarking on this kind of challenge seems daunting.

The idea behind *Bible60* is to set out for readers passages from Scripture which will lead them through the story of the Bible in 60 days. I had already written and presented a course for CWR called The Bible in a Day, for those who want an overview in four and a half hours, so I was able to use the thinking behind that course in the putting together of this book.

Each day includes a chapter or two from the Bible, with comments from me, and requires just 20 minutes to complete. My aim is to help readers understand the sections of Scripture selected, in the context of the overall story of God's Word, and especially the way that the Old Testament continually points to the New.

Bible60 was a joy to write, as I had the privilege of looking afresh at God's wonderful redeeming purposes for the world. These purposes find their fulfilment, of course, in Jesus, whose life demonstrates the love and goodness of God and provides the way for us all to know and love Him.

God's story in
60 snapshots

bible60

Andy Peck
CWR

I would love to think that readers of *Bible60* might fall in love with God all over again, so that they can't help sharing the news of His love with others.

Bible60: God's story in 60 snapshots
By Andy Peck
£7.99
Also available in eBook/Kindle formats

Order using the form at the back or online at
www.cwr.org.uk

UPCOMING COURSES TO HELP YOU ENGAGE WITH THE BIBLE:

THE BIBLE IN A DAY
Thurs 25 April 2013
Led by Andy Peck

THE BIG STORY
Tues-Sat 28 May – 1 June 2013
Led by Philip Greenslade

BIBLE DISCOVERY COURSES
Led by Philip Greenslade
- **'The Pebble Who Became a Rock' (The apostle Peter**)
  Tues-Thurs 7-9 May 2013
  At Pilgrim Hall
- **'Famous Last Words' (2 Timothy)**
  Fri-Sun 21-23 June 2013

Unless otherwise stated, all the above courses take place
at Waverley Abbey House, Surrey.
For full details/to book, **visit www.cwr.org.uk** or call **+44 (0)1252 784719**

Where God puts the emphasis

FOR READING & MEDITATION - HEBREWS 9:11-28

'... he entered the Most Holy Place once for all by his own blood,
having obtained eternal redemption.' (v.12)

We must meditate a little further on that wondrous
moment when Jesus revealed Himself to His disciples
as the Paschal Lamb and gave them clear and definite
instructions for His own memorial service. Reflect with
me on the deep importance of what He was saying. His
memorial was not to be a single occasion, like our modern-
day memorial services – the final tribute of loved ones and
friends – but it was to be a regular meal, or service, or both.
He told them also that He desired this act of memorial to
be repeated: 'Do this in remembrance of me.'

**FURTHER
STUDY**

Heb. 10:1-23

1. Contrast
Christ's
sacrifice with
that of bulls.

2. Why can
we appear
before God
confidently?

What were they to do? They were to follow His
actions and use the words He Himself had used
when He had broken the bread. I always feel
myself that something is missing in a Communion
service when there is any departure from the
act of taking, breaking, blessing, identifying and
sharing the bread and the wine. But what do the
bread and wine signify? The words Jesus spoke on
that night make it crystal clear; of the bread, He
said, 'This is my body given for you', and of the
wine, 'This cup is the new covenant in my blood,
which is poured out for you.'

John Stott said of this moment, 'The bread did
not stand for His living body as He reclined with them at
the table, but His body as it was shortly to be "given" for
them in death. Similarly, the wine did not stand for His
blood as it flowed in His veins while He spoke to them, but
His blood which was shortly to be poured out for them in
death.' It is clear that it is not so much by His life, but by
His death, that Jesus wishes to be remembered. His life is
important, but much more His death. It has accomplished
so much for us.

**O God, help me ever to put the emphasis where You have put
it, not so much on my Saviour's life, spotless and exemplary
though it was, but on His sacrificial and atoning death. I ask this
in and through His peerless and precious name. Amen.**

FOR READING & MEDITATION - GALATIANS 6:1-15

'May I never boast except in the cross of our Lord Jesus Christ ...' (v.14)

We continue meditating on the fact that although the life of our Lord was supremely important, the place where God puts the highest emphasis is on His sacrificial and atoning death. Modern-day theologians who bypass the death of Christ and focus instead on such things as His exemplary life, His powerful words, His great miracles and so on, have their priorities all wrong. The emphasis which Jesus placed on His own death shows quite clearly that He regarded this as central to His purpose in coming to the world. Not that His exemplary life and character have no purpose – they most certainly do – but had He not died on the cross, then we would never have known what it means to be 'saved'.

One commentator puts it like this: 'The Lord's Supper, which was instituted by Jesus, and which is the only regular commemorative act authorised by Him, dramatises neither His birth nor His life, neither His words nor His works, but only His death.' It was by His death that He wished above all else to be remembered. You see, then, how essential the cross is to Christianity. In a day and an age when religionists are attempting to turn the spotlight away from the cross and focus instead on the life and words of Jesus, we must do everything in our power to proclaim the centrality of the cross. No cross – no Christianity; it is as simple as that. I take my stand – and I pray that you do too – with the hymnist who said:

FURTHER STUDY

Rom. 1:16-17; 1 Cor. 1:17-30

1. What is the power of the cross?

2. How do people regard the message of the cross?

Forbid it, Lord, that I should boast
Save in the death of Christ my Lord
All the vain things that charm me most
I sacrifice them to his blood.'

Isaac Watts (1674–1748)

O God my Father, I am so glad that even though I cannot fathom all the mystery of the cross, I can take hold of its saving power. It is sometimes darkness to my intellect, but sunshine to my heart. Thank You, Father. Amen.

Getting the 'me' into Calvary

FOR READING & MEDITATION – GALATIANS 2:15-21

'... the Son of God, who loved me and gave himself for me.' (v.20)

Before we leave the Upper Room and go down with Jesus into Gethsemane, we draw one more concluding lesson from what went on in that memorable first Communion service. It concerns the need for each one of us personally to apply and appropriate the death of Christ for ourselves. If, as we have been saying, it was in the Upper Room that Jesus gave to His disciples an advance dramatisation of His death on the cross, it is important that we see further what this was designed to convey.

The celebration of that first Communion did not just involve Jesus, but it involved all the disciples also. Christ initiated it, but the others took part in it as well. They could hardly have failed to get the message that it was not enough for the bread to be broken and the cup of wine to be handed to them – they had to eat and drink and thus appropriate it for themselves. They were not spectators – they were participants.

FURTHER STUDY

John 3:16-21,36;
Rom. 10:8-13

1. What happens to those who reject Christ?

2. Who can be saved?

What does all this say to us? It says that the death of Christ is the means by which we are saved, but we will not be saved until we receive and appropriate for ourselves the sacrifice He made for us on the cross. This is extremely important, for there are many this Easter who, when they are reminded of Christ's death on the cross, will think that because of that, they are automatically forgiven. That is not so. Unless we do as John Wesley said, and get the 'me' into the cross – Christ died for me – and personally receive His forgiveness by an appropriating act of faith, then the tragic situation is this – it will be as if He never died for us.

O Father, thank You for reminding me that it is only as I appropriate what Christ did for me on Calvary that I am saved. I have seen it - may millions more come to know it this Easter time. In Jesus' name I pray. Amen.

'The agony in the Garden'

FOR READING & MEDITATION - EZEKIEL 23:32-34

'You will be filled with drunkenness and sorrow, the cup of ruin and desolation ...' (v.33)

Supper is now over and, after singing, Jesus and His band of disciples make their way down into the Kidron Valley to a little olive orchard known as the Garden of Gethsemane. It was evidently a favourite retreat for Jesus, for John comments that He often met there with His disciples (John 18:2). Here something takes place which many have come to call 'the agony in the Garden'. It is clear from the record that Jesus is in great distress of soul, as on three separate occasions He prays a similar prayer: 'My Father, if it is possible, may this cup be taken from me. Yet not as I will, but as you will' (Matt. 26:39).

What is this 'cup' which Jesus is talking about here? Is He recoiling from the thought of the physical suffering He is about to endure – the awful torture and agony of the cross? Possibly so. This prospect would likely bring deep distress to the soul. In Luke 22:43-44, we read that an angel came to strengthen Jesus, and yet, even after this, He was still in anguish, and He prayed with increased fervour.

Perhaps also something deeper than the thought of physical or even mental suffering was striking deep into His soul. The cup from which He shrank symbolised not just the physical pain of being crucified and the mental distress of being humiliated and despised, but also the spiritual agony of bearing the sins of the world. As Jesus looked into that cup and saw the temporary spiritual break with His Father that would happen on the cross, His soul may have recoiled in horror. You see, it was not the fear of death that caused Him such agony, but the awful prospect of being separated from the One to whom He had been joined throughout all eternity.

FURTHER STUDY

Psa. 22:1-18;
Luke 22:39-46

1. How did David foresee Christ's agony?

2. What happened after the angel strengthened Jesus?

Blessed Lord, as I contemplate Your suffering in the Garden of Gethsemane, I feel like bowing in the dust. If my sin brought such pain to You, then how can I ever sin again? Please give me the grace to live wholly for You. Amen.

He drained the cup

FOR READING & MEDITATION - MATTHEW 26:36-46

'... if it is not possible for this cup to be taken away unless I drink it, may your will be done.' (v.42)

We look once again on this Maundy Thursday at that lonely figure of our Lord in Gethsemane's Garden – sweating, prostrate, overwhelmed with grief and asking His heavenly Father that, if possible, He be spared the drinking of the cup. Each of the three prayers He prayed began in a similar way: 'My Father, if it is possible ...'

Although, in theory, everything is possible to God, this was something which Jesus recognised as being part of God's will. It was God's purpose to save us from sin, and to save us in a way that would impart to us His righteousness.

FURTHER STUDY

Psa. 69:1-36;
Matt. 27:34

1. Describe the psalmist's feelings.

2. How does the psalm foretell Jesus' experience?

But this would be impossible without the substitutionary death of the Saviour. No one else could have borne our sins. There have been many who would have been willing to die for the sins of the world, but no one who was worthy to die. As the hymn so beautifully puts it:

*There was no other good enough
To pay the price of sin
He only could unlock the gate
Of heaven and let us in.*

Cecil F. Alexander (1818–1895)

So despite Jesus' agonising prayer, the cup was not taken from Him. We have noted that each of His prayers began in a similar way: 'My Father, if it is possible ...' Now we recognise that they each ended with submission to His Father's will. Personally, I am so grateful to Jesus – and so, I am sure, are you – that on that dark night long ago, He put that bitter cup to His lips *and drained it dry.*

My Saviour and my God, how can I sufficiently thank You for drinking that bitter cup of sin so that I could drink the better cup of salvation. My gratitude and appreciation just won't go into words. Amen.

'Darkness at noon'

FOR READING & MEDITATION - MATTHEW 27:45-54

'From the sixth hour until the ninth hour darkness came over all the land.' (v.45)

We come now to another Good Friday and turn from gazing on Jesus in the Garden to His agony on the cross. If the anticipation of bearing the wrath of God against sin was so terrible, then what must the reality have been like? We can only glimpse in some small way what Jesus passed through in that grim ordeal on Golgotha by examining the deeply suggestive text which is before us today: 'darkness came over all the land'.

A strange and eerie darkness swept over Jerusalem on that awful day when Jesus was crucified, which seems to have lasted for three hours – from the sixth hour (noon) to the ninth hour (3pm). What a contrast there was between our Saviour's birth and His death. As Douglas Webster puts it, 'At the birth of the Son of God, there was brightness at midnight; at the death of the Son of God, there was darkness at noon.'

What was the purpose of this strange phenomenon? I think myself it was the outward symbol of the spiritual darkness that was enveloping Jesus as 'He himself bore our sins in his body on the tree' (1 Pet. 2:24). What is darkness, in biblical symbolism, but separation from God, who is light and in whom there is no darkness at all (1 John 1:5)? The term 'outer darkness' is an expression that Jesus once used to describe hell, since it is absolute and utter exclusion from the light of God's presence. Hold this thought in your mind as you go through the day – at Calvary our Lord, in some mysterious way, plunged into that 'outer darkness' and experienced, on our behalf, the awful terror of temporary separation from God.

FURTHER STUDY

1 John 1:5-9; 2:1-11

1. How does John contrast light and dark?

2. Why might we be in darkness?

Blessed Lord Jesus, as I stand before Your cross and see something more of what it meant for You, I see something more of what it means for me. And I bow myself down. Thank You, dear Saviour. Thank You! Amen.

The cry of dereliction

FOR READING & MEDITATION - PSALM 22:1-31

'My God, my God, why have you forsaken me?' (v.1)

Today, in the interim between Good Friday and Easter Sunday, we spend another day meditating on the cross. When Jesus emerged from the darkness that enveloped Him, He made a strange and puzzling statement: 'My God, my God, why have you forsaken me?' These words have come to be called by many theologians and Bible students, 'the cry of dereliction'.

What is the explanation of these anguished words? Everyone agrees that Jesus was quoting Psalm 22, but not everyone agrees as to the purpose of the quotation. Some say it was a cry of unbelief and despair – He was disappointed that His Father had not rescued Him from the awful horror of the cross. Others say it was a cry of loneliness – He was not really forsaken by God, but He *felt* forsaken. Another school of thought sees the words as a cry of victory, saying that as the psalm ends in a spirit of triumph and conquest, Jesus had in mind the end and not just the beginning of the passage.

FURTHER STUDY

2 Chron. 24:20;
2 Cor. 5:17-21;
Heb. 13:5

1. What is the 'Divine Exchange'?

2. What can we say confidently?

I prefer myself to accept the words as they stand and believe them to be indicative of the fact that, due to the need for Christ to taste the full penalty of sin, an actual and dreadful separation voluntarily accepted by both the Father and the Son took place between them at the cross. Jesus not only felt forsaken – He was forsaken. It had to be if the Son was to taste fully the final consequence of human sin. And what is that final consequence? Solemnly I say it – separation from God. Jesus quoted the scripture from Psalm 22 as He quoted other scriptures – not because He was bewildered, stunned or confused, but because He knew and believed He was fulfilling it.

O Jesus, my Lord and my God, I stand in awe at Your sacrificial love. I am on holy ground. There is nothing I can do to repay You for what You have done for me. My best offering is my life for Your service. Amen.

Bible Discovery: The Pebble who Became a Rock
Led By Philip Greenslade

Tracking Peter's faith journey from big fisherman to founding apostle, as recorded in the Gospels, Acts and 1 and 2 Peter, we will be led to revalue the man described by New Testament scholar Martin Hengel as 'the underestimated apostle', and we will be encouraged and challenged by his amazing story.

Venue: Pilgrim Hall
Tues–Thurs 7–9 May
£215 Residential/£162 Non-residential

Bible Discovery Weekend – Famous Last Words
Led by Philip Greenslade

Often acknowledged as the apostle Paul's 'last word' and final testimony, his Second Letter to Timothy is also perhaps his most personal epistle. He writes from a pastoral heart with tough love to instruct, inspire and invigorate the young pastor, Timothy, who has been his 'son' in the faith. 'Every part of Scripture is God-breathed and useful one way or another – showing us truth, exposing our rebellion, correcting our mistakes, training us to live God's way.'

Venue: Waverley Abbey House
Fri–Sun 21–23 June
£215 Residential/£162 Non-residential
Early Bird Prices £193.50 Residential/£145.80 Non-residential (Up to 29 March 2013)

For further info/To book: **www.cwr.org.uk** or call **+44 (0)1252 784719**.
Prices and dates correct at the time of printing.

Introduction to Biblical Care and Counselling

Led by Angie Coombes, Richard Laws and team

This five-day foundation course is an ideal way to begin learning how to put your desire to help people into effective practice. You will be encouraged to reflect on your own life in the light of the biblical model presented, before using the principles to help others. Our approach has transformed the lives of so many who have been on this course. Key features include: the biblical basis for pastoral care and counselling, how to deal with life's basic issues successfully and essential facts every people-helper should know.

Venue: Waverley Abbey House
Mon–Fri 18–22 March, Mon–Fri 12–16 August, Mon–Fri 18–22 November
Venue: Pilgrim Hall
Mon–Fri 10–14 June
£450 Residential/£350 Non-residential

Pastoral Care in the Local Church

*Led by Stuart Pascall, Lynn Penson
and the CWR Tutor Team*

Lives and communities are
transformed as people feel cared
for. Come with us and explore God's
passionate heart for caring, God's
affirming call, God's equipping grace
and God's effective people. Whether
leading or being involved in a pastoral
care team, or just exploring your
pastoral gifting, this course will
enlarge your vision of the Church's
calling to pastoral care. It will help you
develop your caring skills, whether
using them individually or as part of a
wider team.

Venue: Waverley Abbey House
Mon–Fri 11–15 March
£450 Residential/£350 Non-residential

*'This course
is to be highly
recommended;
inspirational
practical teaching
in a beautiful,
relaxed and friendly
environment.'*

The Big Story
– Genesis to Revelation
Led by Philip Greenslade

Join us on this exciting course and explore with gifted Bible teacher Philip Greenslade the narrative of Scripture to gain understanding of the deep underlying structure of the Bible and the overarching redemptive strategy of God. This includes, how the important pieces of the Bible narrative fit together and how our personal stories relate to God's bigger story.

Venue: Waverley Abbey House
Tues–Sat 28 May – 1 June
£450 Residential/£350 Non-residential

God's Questions
Led by Philip Greenslade

For more information and to book places, visit www.cwr.org.uk/training or call +44 (0)1252 784719

Venue: Waverley Abbey House
Mon–Wed 23–25 September
£235 Residential/£180 Non-residential
Early Bird Prices £211.50 Residential/
£162 Non-residential (up to 1 July 2013)

Future Bible Discovery Weekend
Venue: Waverley Abbey House
Fri–Sun 8–10 November

'A wonderful experience; clear, challenging, helpful and inspiring teacing; great company, food and rest.'

WOMEN'S WEEKENDS

Women's weekends offer time and space to enjoy the company of God and others, to listen, laugh and share, to reflect creatively and pray in the beautiful surroundings.

Springs of Life

Led by Nicky-Sue Terry and Ros Derges

What we hold in our hearts affects the way we experience life, and Jesus wants us to enjoy an abundant life. What are our hearts like? What is it that we are to guard? We can pray with the psalmist, 'Search me, O God, and know my heart' (Psalm 139:23). Jesus knew people's hearts, and His teaching inspires us to develop hearts that are pure, generous, forgiving and loving. Like His, our hearts are to reflect something of God's heart. Join us as we explore the richness of life that our hearts can hold and impart, as we seek to become women after God's own heart.

Venue: Waverley Abbey House
Fri-Sun 26-28 April
£185 Residential/£135 Non-residential

Preparation for Marriage

*Led by Mick & Lynette Brooks
with Lynn & Andrew Penson*

Build a firm biblical foundation as you consider the nature of Christian marriage, love and sexuality. With help from the Myers-Briggs Type Indicator®, develop mutual understanding and learn to handle conflict and avoid marriage breakdown, as you identify the strengths, weaknesses and potential stress points in your relationship.

Venue: Waverley Abbey House
Fri–Sun 1-3 March
£410 Residential per couple
(£205 per person if being paid for separately)

Marriage on Track

Led by Lynn & Andrew Penson

Enjoy a weekend together in beautiful surroundings offering the opportunity to consider what Christian marriage means and explore topics such as communication, handling conflict, sexual intimacy, expressing love and understanding your partner with the help of the Myers-Briggs Type Indicator®. Celebrate your marriage with a romantic dinner *a deux* on Saturday evening!

Venue: Waverley Abbey House
Fri–Sun 11-13 October
£410 Residential per couple
Early Bird Price £369 (up to 19 July 2013)

Certificate in Counselling Supervision - Stages 1 and 2
Led by Heather Churchill

The overall aim of the course is to equip delegates with the necessary skills and knowledge to provide supervisory support and guidance to counsellors in clinical practice. The course will assist delegates to:

- Understand the purpose and role of supervision
- Consider ethical and legal responsibilities of supervision, including boundaries and contract issues
- Understand the theories and models of supervising both individuals and groups
- Develop the necessary skills to establish an effective working alliance
- Evaluate the supervisory process, including their own practice of supervision
- Understand life cycles of groups and group dynamics in group supervision

Venue: Waverley Abbey House
Stage 1: Mon-Tues 4-5 March
Stage 2: Mon-Tues 20-21 May
£475 Residential/£420 Non-residential (Includes both Stage 1 and Stage 2)

Women's Weekend
- In the Palm of His Hand
*Led by Lynn Penson
and Beverley Shepherd*

What part of the body do we use to welcome, to give, to restrain, to love, to create, to bring healing, to guide, to help? Our hands. Scripture uses wonderful pictures of God's hands as doing all this and much more beside. During this week we will be exploring what it means to be held secure in, and sustained by, the loving hands of God and how we can become 'God's hands' to others. This is a wonderful opportunity for you to draw closer to God and be renewed. You will enjoy meeting new friends and the good food too!

Venue: Pilgrim Hall
Fri-Sun 5-7 July
£185 Residential/£135 Non-residential
Early Bird Prices £166.50 Residential/£121.50 Non-residential (Up to 12 April 2013)

Woman to Woman
Led by Lynn Penson and team

This unique course is designed for women of all ages who want to help and minister to other women, whether on a one-to-one basis, leading a small group or with responsibility for a church or area-wide group. The course is brimming with opportunities to learn and grow as you understand more about yourself and explore your gifts, vision, spirituality and abilities. The weekend includes: establishing biblical foundations, developing visions and goals, identifying your spiritual gifting and much more.

Venue: Pilgrim Hall
Mon-Fri 17-21 June
£450 Residential/£350 Non-residential
Early Bird Prices £405 Residential/£315 Non-residential (Up to 25 March 2013)

'It has been helpful in my own personal walk with the Lord, and has provided a toolbox with which to go and help others.'

OTHER WOMEN'S WEEKENDS IN 2013

Pilgrim Hall:
Fri-Sun 25-27 October
£185 Residential/£135 Non-residential
Early Bird Prices £166.50 Residential/£121.50 Non-residential (Up to 2 August 2013)

Waverley Abbey House:
Fri-Sun 29 November – 1 December
£185 Residential/£135 Non-residential
Early Bird Prices £166.50 Residential/£121.50 Non-residential (Up to 6 September 2013)

'I am alive! I am alive!'

FOR READING & MEDITATION - JOHN 20:1-18; REVELATION 1:18

'I am the Living One; I was dead, and behold I am alive for ever and ever!' (Rev. 1:18)

On the third day after Christ had died on the cross, He was miraculously brought back to life again, and today it is this event which millions of Christians around the world are joyfully celebrating. Historians tell us that at the Battle of Hastings in 1066, there was a joyous moment when the Norman invaders were about to be overcome. For long hours they had striven without success to storm Harold's stockades, and they were beginning to get weary and lose heart. A rumour began to spread among them which almost led to panic – a rumour which reported that their leader, William, had been slain. As soon as William heard it, he jumped on his horse and rode up and down among the ranks shouting, 'I am alive! I am alive! I am alive!'

What a graphic picture this is of Jesus on the first Easter Day. Many of Christ's followers who were not present at the cross would have heard the sad news that He had been crucified and His body laid in a tomb. The report of His death would have been carried miles beyond the city of Jerusalem, and doubtless those who had believed in Him would have been deeply saddened and distressed.

Jesus, however, did not allow the news of His death to discourage His disciples for too long as, a little while later, He flung back from His face the mask of death and announced, first to Mary and then to other chosen disciples, 'I am alive! I am alive! I am alive!' On this, another Easter Day, come with me and peer into the tomb in which Jesus was laid. What do you see? Nothing? Ah – that, I am sure you will agree, is the most marvellous and most sensational 'nothing' the world has ever known.

FURTHER STUDY

Luke 24:1-12;
John 20:24-31

1. How did the disciples initially respond?

2. How did Jesus settle their doubts?

Lord Jesus, thankful as I am for the empty tomb, that is not the only thing that convinces me You are alive. The greatest evidence is that You are alive within my heart – and for that I am eternally thankful. Amen.

Victory all the way

FOR READING & MEDITATION - COLOSSIANS 2:1-15

'... he made a public spectacle of them, triumphing over them
by the cross.' (v.15)

We spend another day reflecting on the wonder of Jesus'
resurrection. Let's pause to consider now how Christ's
death and resurrection are connected, for many Christians
have a sentimental but not a connected understanding of
these two great and momentous events. It is popularly
believed that the resurrection is the way by which God
turned the defeat of Good Friday into a glorious victory.
But that is a part truth. The death of Jesus on that first Good
Friday was not a defeat but a victory, and the resurrection
is that victory endorsed, demonstrated and proclaimed.

**FURTHER
STUDY**

Acts 17:30-34;
1 Cor. 15:1-23

1. What was the
decisive point in
Paul's message?

2. Why could
our faith be
futile and
our belief be
in vain?

The apostle Peter, in his sermon on the Day of
Pentecost, said, 'It was impossible for death to
keep its hold on him' (Acts 2:24). It was possible
for Him to die, but not possible for Him to be held
by death. Why? Because on the cross, death had
already been defeated. The evil principalities and
powers which had been conquered by His death
on the cross were, at the moment of resurrection,
put under His feet and made subject to Him
(Eph. 1:20–23).

Some Christians present Christ as a living Lord,
but place no emphasis on His atoning death,
while others talk about His atoning death but
fail to focus on His resurrection. The two events
belong together and exclusion of one diminishes the other.
Nothing would have been accomplished by Jesus' death if
He had not been raised from it, and nothing would have
been accomplished by His resurrection if He had not dealt
with death and defeated it *on the cross*. Good Friday was
as much a victory as Easter Sunday.

**My Father and my God, help me not to separate what You have
joined together. Deepen my understanding of the cross and
resurrection so that I might experience even more dynamically
their power in my life. In Jesus' name. Amen.**

A continuous practice

FOR READING & MEDITATION - ACTS 2:38-47

'They devoted themselves to the apostles' teaching and to the
fellowship, to the breaking of bread ...' (v.42)

Today we ask ourselves: how faithfully, after the
cross and resurrection, did the disciples practice
Jesus' instructions concerning the regular celebration
of Communion? The chapter before us today makes it
clear that within weeks of the Last Supper, the disciples
had taught the converts the importance of this event,
for we read, 'They devoted themselves to the apostles'
teaching and to the fellowship, to *the breaking of bread*
and to prayer'. Again we read in verse 46, 'Every day they
continued to meet together in the temple courts. They
broke bread in their homes and ate together with
glad and sincere hearts' (my emphases).

It would appear from these verses that the
actual practice of celebrating Communion was
as part of a fellowship meal, but later the Church
came to set aside a specific time in which they
focused exclusively on remembering their Lord's
sacrifice for them on Calvary: 'On the first day
of the week we came together to break bread'
(Acts 20:7). By the time the first letter to the
Corinthians was written (around AD 55), it is
clear that the celebration of Communion was a regular
practice in the Corinthian community, as evidenced by the
phrase, 'The cup of thanksgiving for which we give thanks
... the bread that we break' (1 Cor. 10:16).

What the Church of the first century practised ought to
be the practice of the Church of the twenty-first century.
Jesus said, 'Do this in remembrance of me,' and so, until
He returns to take us to be with Him, we are to obey His
command and make this feast a continuous practice. Jesus'
sacrifice is of too great importance not to be regularly
brought to mind and celebrated.

FURTHER STUDY

Luke 24:13-35

1. What happened when the stranger broke bread?

2. How did it affect them?

**O Father, I see that if the Church misses its step here then
it will miss it all along the way. Help us to be faithful to Your
commands, for they are there for our benefit and for Your glory.
In Jesus' name we ask it. Amen.**

Why Paul?

FOR READING & MEDITATION - 1 CORINTHIANS 11:23-26
'For I received from the Lord what I also passed on to you ...' (v.23)

We come today to the only passage in the epistles where the purpose and meaning of the Communion table is expounded and explained. At first, it seems a little strange that this task is given to the apostle Paul, especially when we remember that he was not present at Jesus' last meal with the disciples. Where did Paul get his deep understanding of Holy Communion? From one or more of the original band of disciples? No – he got it directly from Jesus Himself: '*I received from the Lord* what I also pass on to you' (my emphasis).

FURTHER STUDY

Acts 22:1-3;
1 Cor. 9:19-23;
Gal. 1:11-24

1. What was special about Paul's background and character?

2. What was special about Paul's understanding?

But why was Paul chosen to be the one to give the only exposition of the meaning of Communion in the whole of the epistles? Why not Simon Peter, or John? I believe myself that the reason for this is because Paul had been given a special commission to bring the gospel to the Gentiles (Rom. 15:16) and to him also had been given the revelation of the true nature of the Christian Church (Eph. 3:1-11).

Two things emerge from this – one, that Paul was specially gifted to make clear to the Gentiles the significance of Old Testament truths that could easily elude them, and two, the great apostle was able, more than any of the other New Testament writers, to expound the truths that related particularly to the Church. As Holy Communion was intended by Jesus to be a corporate and not an individual celebration – something done within the context of the Body of Christ – then who better to instruct and apply that truth than the great apostle to the Gentiles?

Gracious Father, I am so thankful that You gave Your servant Paul an inspired insight into the Communion. May the same Spirit who inspired him be in my heart as I ponder these insights over the next few days. Amen.

The five c's of the Communion

FOR READING & MEDITATION - 1 CORINTHIANS 11:26-34

'For whenever you eat this bread and drink this cup, you proclaim the Lord's death ...' (v.26)

We said yesterday that Paul's exposition of the meaning of Communion contained in I Corinthians 11:23–34 is the only passage in the whole of the epistles where the meaning of Holy Communion is unfolded and explained. For this reason I intend to put it under a spiritual microscope day by day and draw out of it the lessons we need to learn. Firstly, let me say that as this is a devotional study read by people of all denominations, I do not intend to enter into some of the more controversial issues, but to focus on those things on which all (or at least most) Christians can agree.

Five clear aspects are seen in the Lord's Supper, and keeping these in view whenever we sit or kneel before the 'holy table' will, I believe, enable us to enter more fully into the meaning of this precious and sacred act. Firstly, the service of Communion is a corporate act in which the whole Christian community is expected to participate. Secondly, it is a commemorative act in which we focus on remembering Jesus' sacrificial and atoning death. Thirdly, it is a service in which the concept of covenant is highlighted. Fourthly, it is an act of celebration entered into with joy and thanksgiving. And fifthly, it is an act of commitment in which we dedicate ourselves more fully to representing our Master in a hostile and often Christ-rejecting world.

These five aspects, when understood and kept in view as we come to the Lord's Table, will, I believe, help to turn what can be a routine monotonous event into a momentous one. We owe it to God and ourselves to draw out from the Communion all that Father God has put into it.

FURTHER STUDY

Gen. 14:11-20;
Isa. 55:1-7

1. How did Abram experience a type of communion?

2. What is God's invitation?

Jesus, my Lord and Master, help me understand that the Communion service is not just a ritual but something that is close to Your heart. You initiated it - teach me how to appreciate it. For Your own dear name's sake. Amen.

A 'together' fellowship

FOR READING & MEDITATION - ACTS 20:1-12

'On the first day of the week we came together to break bread.' (v.7)

We said yesterday that at least five clear aspects can be seen in the Communion, and an understanding of these will help to enrich the times we spend together at the Lord's Table. The first thing we must understand about the Communion is that it is a corporate act. God never intended that we should partake of the Lord's Supper alone in the privacy of our own room. We 'come together' (1 Cor. 11:20) in order to celebrate it.

Scripture calls us to come together to observe the Lord's Supper. Sometimes you hear Christians using the word 'communion' to describe their times of private prayer and fellowship with the Lord, but the word 'communion', when applied to the Lord's Supper, means more than that – it means fellowship with other Christians also. If you want an interesting evening in your Bible, go through the Acts of the Apostles and observe the number of times the word 'together' or its synonyms occur. You will come to the conclusion that the Early Church was a very 'together' fellowship.

FURTHER STUDY

Acts 2:42-47;
Heb. 10:23-25

1. What can we learn from the Early Church?

2. What should we not neglect?

Of course, those who are ill in hospital or housebound are unable to attend Communion services. Community can be found, however, when another Christian visits with bread and wine, and Communion can be shared where they are. At the Communion table, we not only share in Christ, but we share in each other. As I have said on numerous occasions in these pages over the years – everyone who belongs to Christ belongs to everyone else who belongs to Christ. There is no such thing as a solitary Christian.

O God, teach me the value of sharing my life with You, but also with others – for this is truly living. May sharing in Communion with others be part of that. In Jesus' name. Amen.

FOR READING & MEDITATION - 1 CORINTHIANS 11:17-22

'When you come together, it is not the Lord's Supper you eat ...'
(v.20)

We saw yesterday, that Scripture calls us to join together in order to observe the Lord's Supper. This means more than just the physical act of coming together – it involves a spiritual coming together also.

Paul's exposition of the Communion is preceded by strong words which he felt obliged to speak to the church because of certain irregularities that were allowed to go on in their midst. Apparently, in the church at Corinth, the act of remembering the Lord's death was preceded by a 'love feast' – a communal meal to which all would contribute. Somehow the meal had become degraded into an act whereby the rich would sit to one side and enjoy their sumptuous provisions, while the poor would find a separate place to eat their meagre fare. Then, immediately after the eating of this meal, came the celebration of the Lord's Supper.

Paul was concerned because the evident lack of love that was demonstrated at the 'love feast' spilled over into the act of Communion and thus the two things contradicted one another. What should have been an act of communion was really nothing more than an act of collaboration. They sat together, but their hearts did not belong to one another. They came together physically, but they did not come together spiritually.

The problem that existed in the Corinthian church is with us in some sections of Christ's Church today. Believers meet together to celebrate the Lord's Supper, but never experience true communion. Thus, sadly, it cannot be said of them as it was said of the church after Pentecost: 'the company of believers was of one heart and soul' (Acts 4:32, Amplified Bible).

FURTHER STUDY

James 2:1-17;
Jude 1-16

1. What is necessary for true communion?

2. What blemishes did Jude highlight?

O God, sweep through Your Church by Your Holy Spirit so that we may experience true communion. Break down all barriers between us, so that we might come together with one heart and one soul. For the glory of Your precious Son. Amen.

The People's Pilgrim

His seminal work, *The Pilgrim's Progress*, has become the world's second most printed book, with the Bible at number one. This February, CWR published a new biography of John Bunyan, and here we talk to its author, Peter Morden, about the remarkable life and impact of 'The People's Pilgrim'.

[CWR:] What drew you to write a biography of John Bunyan?

[Peter Morden:] I have always been fascinated by *The Pilgrim's Progress*. It is such an extraordinary book, full of vivid detail and so relevant to our own 'pilgrimage' with God. But as I learnt more about Bunyan himself, I began to realise his own journey from rebellious youth to popular Christian writer was no less fascinating and challenging.

What was Bunyan's impact in his own day?

It was significant. By the time of his death he was well known as a preacher and *The Pilgrim's Progress* was being talked about on street corners and in homes across the length and breadth of the land. By the nineteenth century, however, *The Pilgrim's Progress* was known across the globe, having been translated into hundreds of languages and dialects. Other books such as *The Holy War* were avidly read too.

Bunyan was more popular than Shakespeare!
People were also interested in his life, devouring
biographies which told of his poor background,
his deep faith in God, his preaching and the
persecution he endured.

What is the one thing about Bunyan's life which has impacted you most?

Bunyan's love for his Lord, love for people and
practical focus have a huge amount to teach
us today. After each chapter of the book I have
included two sections, 'Going Further' and 'Your
Own Journey' to help us apply different lessons
to our own lives. However, much as Bunyan has
inspired, challenged and encouraged me, the
overriding impression having finished the book
concerns the amazing character of God. He is
able to take someone from humble beginnings,
lead them, protect them and shape them for
service, working through all circumstances
for His glory! I hope readers are left with the
same impression, and that through *The People's
Pilgrim* they learn something about Bunyan but
even more about the God he served.

*John Bunyan –
The People's Pilgrim*
By Peter Morden
£9.99
Available February 2013

Order using the form at the back
or online at www.cwr.org.uk

The *koinonia*

FOR READING & MEDITATION - 1 CORINTHIANS 1:1-9

'God, who has called you into fellowship [*koinonia*] with his Son
Jesus Christ our Lord, is faithful.' (v.9)

We ended yesterday with the thought that some
churches come together to celebrate the Lord's Supper
but never really experience communion. The best word to
describe the rich spiritual relationships which Christ looks
for between believers is the Greek word *koinonia* – literally
'fellowship'.

This fellowship, however, goes deeper than mere
'mateyness' or sociability. In the words of George Fox, 'The
church experiences a relationship where they seek to know
each other in that which is eternal.' Other relationships let
us know each other in that which is temporal; the
relationship we have with one another in Christ
lets us know each other at our deepest depths
and 'in that which is eternal'. This thought is
expressed beautifully in these words:

**FURTHER
STUDY**

Ruth 1:1-22

1. Describe
Orpah's
relationship
with Naomi.

2. Contrast
Ruth's
relationship
with Naomi.

*'Oh, without spoken words, low breathing stole
Of a diviner life from soul to soul
Baptising into one tender thought the whole.*
                                          John Russell Hayes

Without this rich fellowship, the Church is
no different to a fraternity or a club. One of the
reasons why the Christians of the Early Church
'turned the world upside down' was because they had a
clear understanding of their relationship with God and
their relationship to one another. They had a true sense of
community. As someone put it, 'Once, the church was an
incendiary fellowship which changed and challenged the
course of history.' The *koinonia* turned the world upside
down; what difference do we make?

**O Father, I see we are made for the *koinonia* and we are restless
and unhappy until we find it. Let this homesickness of the soul
drive us closer to You and to each other. In Jesus' name we pray.
Amen.**

FOR READING & MEDITATION - 1 JOHN 1:1-10

'... if we walk in the light, as he is in the light, we have fellowship
with one another ...' (v.7)

Today we ask ourselves: where and how can this rich
sense of fellowship and community (*koinonia*) be
cultivated and developed? One place is at the Lord's Table.
The regular celebration of Holy Communion greatly assists
in heightening our sense of community. All gathering
together, of course, contributes to a sense of community,
but the Lord's Table plays a special part in producing that
rich fellowship of which we spoke yesterday.

Gathered around the table on which stand the bread and
wine, we are not only reminded of our oneness in Christ
but the thought is borne in upon us that we are a
community of the cross. The regular exposure of
our minds and spirits to the sight of the emblems
which Jesus chose to perpetuate the memory of
His death brings home to us most vividly that,
having been brought into being by the cross, we
continue to live by and under the cross. All our
perspectives and behaviour are to be governed by
the cross.

Just as the cross enables us to enjoy and
experience a new relationship with God, so
it enables us to enjoy and experience a new
relationship with one another. And if there is one
place where we need to open our lives to the power of the
cross, it is in the area of relationships. 'Christianity,' says Dr
E. Stanley Jones, 'is the science of living well together with
others according to Jesus Christ.' Many of our attempts
to live together in harmony are haphazard; we often do
not follow the principles that flow out of the cross. Let's
commit ourselves to following God's ways, ways which we
find represented in the cross and the Lord's Table.

FURTHER STUDY

Amos 3:3;
1 John 3:11-24

1. What basis
do we have to
walk together?

2. How can
we know
and practise
true love?

O Father, help me so to live that just as I am not outside of Your
fellowship, no one shall be outside of mine. You have made clear
that this is Your will for me; teach me how to make it my will
also. Amen.

Suffering love

FOR READING & MEDITATION - 1 CORINTHIANS 13:1-13

'Love ... takes no account of the evil done to it
[pays no attention to a suffered wrong].' (v.5, Amplified Bible)

We spend one more day on the thought that the Lord's Table is a vivid reminder of the fact that we are a community of people called to live by and under the cross. The bread and wine portray and symbolise not just our togetherness in Christ but that our lives are to be governed and regulated by the cross.

Some prefer to think of themselves as the community of the resurrection rather than the community of the cross, and although the former is true, it should be recognised that the table instituted by Jesus has upon it, not the symbols of the resurrection but the symbols of the cross. The resurrection, as we saw, is part of it – a glorious and integral part – but the main focus is on the cross.

FURTHER STUDY

John 15:9-17;
Eph. 4:25-5:2

1. Where is love most greatly displayed?

2. How can we imitate God?

We pause now to consider this pointed and personal question: are our relationships with one another governed and regulated by the cross? When we eat and drink together at the Lord's Table, are we together physically but poles apart spiritually? Each Christian we relate to has within him or her the possibility of giving us joy or pain. If we relate well together, then the result is joy; if we relate badly, then the result is pain.

It is at this point of pain, however, that a cross becomes inevitable. For what is a cross? It is the point at which love crimsons into suffering. Jesus loved us so much that He was willing to suffer for us. In a similar sense, that is what we must do for each other, for Calvary love is suffering love. It holds on to relationships, no matter how difficult they may be, and suffers when necessary the pain that is sometimes inevitable when people of a different upbringing or a different background meet together.

O Father, You know that sometimes it is not easy to relate to some of my brothers and sisters in the Church, but when pain comes in my relationships, help me to demonstrate the quality of suffering love. In Jesus' name I pray. Amen.

Commanded to come?

FOR READING & MEDITATION - GALATIANS 5:1-15

'You were running a good race. Who cut in on you and kept you from obeying the truth?' (v.7)

Now that we have spent a few days clarifying that one of the aspects of Holy Communion is to emphasise the corporate nature of the Church, we move on to explore the second aspect – commemoration. We are commanded to come together in order to remember Him. Notice what I say – 'commanded to come'. Jesus does not just invite us to His table, but insists on us being there.

Does this sound harsh and demanding? Then keep in mind that when Jesus insists on something, you can be sure that there is a wise and loving purpose behind it. His demands are not like those of an autocrat – they are the demands of One who has our highest interests at heart. If you have difficulty with this, then remember, the One who commands you is the One who was crucified for you. Consider His words once again: 'Do this in remembrance of me.' Note, it says '*Do this*' – not 'I *suggest* you do this', or '*Try* to do this'. We are to commemorate His loving sacrifice.

Some believe that this command was intended to apply only to the original band of disciples and not to the continuing life of the Church. There are two strong arguments that can be brought against this view. Firstly, the word 'do' in the Greek suggests repetition – something to be done again and again and again. Secondly, the words 'I received from the Lord what I also pass on to you' (1 Cor. 11:23) show it to be a command from the Lord for the whole Church. So, in the light of these things and because of Jesus' loving sacrifice for us, let's obey the command and meet around His table to remember Him.

FURTHER STUDY

Matt. 7:24-29;
Luke 22:14-20

1. What are the results of ignoring Jesus' words?

2. Why does Jesus insist on us taking communion?

O Jesus, Your loving demands strike deep into our hearts. When we sense You calling us to obey You, help us not to resist, for we know that You have our best interests at heart. For Your own dear name's sake. Amen.

Lest we forget

FOR READING & MEDITATION - PSALM 103:1-22

'... and forget not all his benefits ...' (v.2)

We continue reflecting on the fact that one of the purposes of Communion is to commemorate Jesus' atoning death on Calvary. Whenever I read the words, 'Do this in remembrance of me', my first thought is how sad it is that we who are redeemed should need a reminder at all. One would think that once we come to Christ and understand just what His death has procured for us, the fact would remain in our consciousness through every moment of the day. But, as we know, such is not the case – we tend to forget.

FURTHER STUDY

Deut. 4:9-10; 8:1-20

1. How may things slip from our hearts?

2. Why may God's blessings cause a problem?

One man speaks bitterly of his memory as 'that traitor' while another refers to it as 'the thing he forgot with'. My mother would never admit that she had a poor memory, but referred to it as 'a good forgettory'. I heard of one man who was lent the same book on seven different occasions without realising that he had read it before. His comment was, 'An excellent book, but the author sometimes repeats himself.'

Of all the forms of forgetfulness, however, infinitely the worst is to forget Christ. To guard against this contingency, Jesus instituted the sacrament, for He knew how the simple ordinance would help to quicken our memory. We look at the bread and wine, and the sight of the emblems triggers our memories and Calvary comes clearly into focus. The infirmity of memory is a contributory factor to our frequent failure to focus on Jesus' death and its meaning for our lives, but the finest antidote to this is regular attendance at the Lord's Table. The feast banishes forgetfulness. We remember, because we are reminded.

O God, I am sad that I should ever need to be reminded of what You did for me on Calvary. But I am glad that You have anticipated my forgetfulness and provided in the bread and wine such an amazing visual aid. Thank You, Father. Amen.

Christ's invisibility

FRI
12 APR

FOR READING & MEDITATION - 1 PETER 1:3-12

'Though you have not seen him, you love him ... (v.8)

Yesterday we saw how the infirmity of memory is a contributory factor to our frequent failure to focus on Jesus' atoning death. Another reason why we can so easily forget our Lord and what He has done for us on the cross is because of His invisibility. We know that He is alive but our eyes never see Him. We do not even have a bust or photograph of Him. No canvas carries His portrait and the Gospels do not give so much as a hint concerning His physical appearance.

Because Jesus is for the present invisible to our gaze, it is sadly easy to overlook His reality. Ian Macpherson puts it thus: 'What we see seems real and what we cannot see, unreal. The visible impinges vividly upon our consciousness; the invisible inclines to recede into oblivion.'

The invisibility of Christ can be one reason why we occasionally forget Jesus – yet it need not be. The Table, with its simple emblems, stimulates the memory; the bread is graphically reminiscent of His flesh; the wine, of His blood. To the devout and reverent imagination, the precious and sacred emblems objectify the reality of the unseen Redeemer, and we recall His atoning death and sacrifice for us. We remember because we are reminded. And when we remember, we can look forward to the day when we will see Jesus face to face. In the words of the hymn:

FURTHER STUDY

2 Cor. 4:16-5:7;
Heb. 11:1-3,23-29

1. Where did Paul fix his gaze?

2. What did Moses see?

> *Only faintly now, I see Him,*
> *With the darkling veil between,*
> *But a blessed day is coming,*
> *When His glory shall be seen.*
>
> *Mrs Frank A. Break (1855–1934)*

Lord Jesus, how can I sufficiently thank You for this simple feast that serves to banish all my forgetfulness. The broken bread and the poured-out wine become the hands that reach out and draw me to Yourself. I am eternally grateful. Amen.

'This feast of memory'

FOR READING & MEDITATION - LUKE 24:13-35

'Jesus was recognised by them when he broke the bread.' (v.35)

Today we look at yet another reason why we can so easily forget Jesus' redemptive sacrifice for us on the cross – the constant pressure of the world around us. As Wordsworth put it, 'The world is too much with us.' The current population of the earth is somewhere in excess of 7 billion inhabitants, but, as someone has put it, 'There is always One more who is never taken account of in any census – the living Christ Himself.'

The people who bustle around us every day of our lives – for some just a few, for others hundreds or thousands –

FURTHER STUDY

Lev. 23:1-44

1. What were the five feasts of the Lord?

2. What did they signify?

have a great influence upon us. We carry within us, albeit subconsciously, their words, their laughter, their tears and even their angry words, gestures and blasphemies. We can see them, hear them and touch them. But the One whom no census recognises is intangible and inaudible. It is natural, therefore, that the people we rub shoulders with day by day, because they are tangible and audible, tend to influence us more than the spiritual realities which we know exist, but which cannot be seen with our physical eyes or heard by our physical ears.

Jesus seems to have anticipated this problem when He appointed for us the Communion table – this wondrous 'feast of memory'. Knowing how the world would impinge upon us and how influential that would be, He ordained that in the life of the Church, there should be regular seasons of remembrance when, with the graphic symbols of His Presence before us, we would deliberately and with set purpose call Him to mind. I have been startled many times, and so I am sure have you, by how powerfully Jesus can make Himself known in the breaking of bread.

O Father, when I see how lovingly You have anticipated my needs and how carefully You have provided for my spiritual development, I am utterly amazed. Such love deserves my total response. I give it - gladly and willingly. Amen.

'Jesus *is* the Atonement'

FOR READING & MEDITATION - PHILIPPIANS 3:1-16

'I want to know Christ and the power of his resurrection and the fellowship of sharing in his sufferings ...' (v.10)

We spend another day meditating on the truth that one of the great purposes of attending the Lord's Supper is to stimulate our memories in the remembrance of Jesus. Indeed, the prescribed actions with the bread and wine (taking, breaking, eating and drinking) make the remembrance vivid and dramatic.

Notice, however, that Jesus does not ask us to remember the date or the place, but *Him*. He does not say, 'Do this in remembrance of my death', although, of course, the fact that He died a redemptive death can never be far from our minds as we eat the bread and drink the wine. I think that what He had in mind when He uttered these words could be paraphrased like this: 'Do this in remembrance of all that I am to you.' It is terribly important that we catch what Jesus intended here, for there are some who focus more on the fact than the Person. Remember, it is not this, that or the other that saves – it is Christ who saves.

When Dr Edwards of Bala, the great Welsh theologian, was busy at his book on the atonement, a thought burst in on him that seemed to set his soul on fire. Jumping up from the desk at which he was sitting, he dashed out into the street, shouting excitedly, 'Jesus *is* the Atonement! Jesus *is* the Atonement!' Then, going back to his study, he wrote, 'This is the Atonement, not the sufferings and not the death, but the person of the Son of God in the sufferings and the death.' This must always be a central focus in our minds whenever we approach the Communion table – not just the time, the date, the deed or the place – but *Him*.

FURTHER STUDY

1 Cor. 1:30;
Col. 1:15-29

1. How has the concept of righteousness become a person?

2. What is Christ's place?

Blessed Lord Jesus, help me not to be so caught up with the events that surround Your death at Calvary that I fail to be caught up with You. Help me to make You central - and all else marginal. For Your own dear name's sake. Amen.

Triggering the memory

'In the future, when your children ask you, "What do these stones mean?" tell them ....' (vv.6-7)

We have been saying that great events must not be forgotten. Doubtless, it was because of this that God commanded the children of Israel to observe the feast of the Passover at the beginning of every new year. It seems remarkable, on the surface of it, that a commemorative event should really be necessary. You would have thought that with such an outstanding event as the deliverance from Egypt in their history, the generations of the children of Israel would have talked about it, not once a year but every day of their lives. Why should they need a visible and concrete reminder of the event in the form of a seven-day feast?

FURTHER STUDY

Deut. 11:8-25;
2 Pet. 1:3-9

1. How were memories to be triggered?

2. What was Peter's concern?

God gave them this instruction because He knew the terrible tendency of the human heart to forget. It is simply astonishing how easily we can blot out from our minds, not only the unpleasant things of the past, but the great and important ones as well. It was because of this that God instructed the children of Israel, after they had miraculously crossed over the Jordan, to build a monument of stones so that future generations would be prompted to ask, 'What do these stones mean?'

One of the most devastating effects of sin is the paralysis it brings to both mind and memory. Dr Martyn Lloyd-Jones said, 'We are so dull and stupid as the result of sin, that we might even forget the death of the Son of God for us, if the Lord Himself had not ordained and commanded that we should meet together and take bread and wine. It is the setting up of the stones in Gilgal once more.'

O Father, I am so grateful for the redemption You have provided through Your Son. And I am grateful, too, that You have planned, through the institution of Holy Communion, to help me never to forget to be grateful. Amen.

Memorial stones

FOR READING & MEDITATION - EXODUS 28:1-14

'... fasten them on the shoulder pieces of the ephod as memorial stones for the sons of Israel.' (v.12)

We must spend one more day meditating on the importance of commemorative acts that help to keep alive in our minds and memories the great events of the past. We suffer so much from the effects of the Fall that we need objective things and tangible reminders – something outside of ourselves – that will lead us, as we saw yesterday, to ask, 'What do these stones mean?'

There are many reasons that could be given for the benefit that comes from commemorating divine acts and events, but perhaps the biggest reason is this – it reminds us of facts. Our security as believers rests not on theories, ideas or suppositions – but *facts*. I have heard some theologians say that we can dispense with the facts of our faith and simply hang on to the teaching that arises out of those facts. This is a subtle and dangerous suggestion and leads to great error. The Exodus of the children of Israel from Egypt was a fact. The daily supply of manna in the wilderness (except on the Sabbath) was a fact. The crossing of the Jordan was a fact.

They are all great and glorious facts – facts of God. The death and resurrection of Jesus Christ is also a fact – something that belongs solidly to history. When the future generations of Israel would ask, 'What do these stones mean?' the reply would be given – something miraculous and wonderful happened here. When, today, the question is asked of us, 'What do the bread and the wine on the Lord's table mean?' the same answer must be given – something miraculous and wonderful happened here.

FURTHER STUDY

Luke 1:1-4;
1 Cor. 15:1-8

1. Why did Luke write his Gospel?

2. What was of first importance to Paul?

My Lord and my God, I am so grateful that I am a partaker of the most miraculous and mighty event this planet ever saw - Jesus' death on Calvary. Help me, through my life and witness, to make the meaning of redemption a little clearer to someone today. In Jesus' name I ask it. Amen.

A new covenant

FOR READING & MEDITATION - HEBREWS 12:18-29

'... to Jesus the mediator of a new covenant ...' (v.24)

We come now to the third aspect of the Communion –
the aspect of covenant. I have met many Christians
over the years who are turned off by the word 'covenant'.
They feel it to be a word that describes the technicalities
of the faith – something to be debated in places of
theological education rather than discussed as part of
everyday discipleship.

Let me say two things about this: firstly, the concept
underlying the biblical word 'covenant' is something even
the youngest Christian can grasp. Secondly, not to grasp

**FURTHER
STUDY**

Gen. 9:1-17;
17:1-14

1. Who initiates
a covenant
between man
and God?

2. What part
do we play
in covenant
with God?

it means you will miss out on the real depth of
meaning that lies behind the Communion. In all
four records given to us of the institution of the
Lord's Supper, we find an allusion to covenant.
Matthew says, 'This is my blood of the covenant'
(Matt. 26:28). Mark uses identical words and Luke
uses similar words. Paul says, 'This cup is the
new covenant in my blood' (1 Cor. 11:25). Notice
particularly Matthew's words: 'This is my blood ...
which is poured out for many *for the forgiveness
of sins*' (my emphasis).

Just think of the fantastic truth that lies
enshrined in these words – through the shedding
of the Saviour's blood, God was taking the initiative
to establish a new pact or 'covenant' with His people, out
of which would come the blessing of forgiveness for sin.
God, of course, had always been *willing* to forgive sin, but
because of its heinous and serious nature, some kind of
'satisfaction' was necessary. The Old Testament sacrifices
could never really take away sin – a new way had to be
found. At the Last Supper, Jesus stood to break the news
that a new way had been found. Hallelujah!

**O God my Father, I am so grateful that You found a way not
to ignore my sin, but to forgive it. And it was not a cheap
forgiveness, but a costly one. It drew blood. All honour and
praise to Your wonderful and mighty name. Amen.**

Awaiting a signature

FOR READING & MEDITATION - JEREMIAH 31:31-37

'The time is coming ... when I will make a new covenant with the house of Israel and with the house of Judah.' (v.31)

Today we ask ourselves the question: what exactly is a covenant? The dictionary meaning of the word signifies a mutual undertaking or agreement between two or more parties, each binding himself to its full obligations. The Bible word for covenant (Greek: *diatheke*), however, does not in itself contain the idea of a joint obligation; it mostly signifies a promise or an undertaking given by a single person.

To understand the idea behind the 'covenant' which Jesus spoke about at the Last Supper, we must again take a brief look at Jewish history. Many centuries before Jesus came, God had entered into a covenant with Abraham, sealed by blood, in which He promised to bless him and bring him into a good and prosperous land (Gen. 15). Later God renewed that covenant with Abraham's descendants – the Israelites – after He had rescued them from slavery in Egypt (Exod. 24).

Hundreds of years after this, in the seventh century BC, when the people had forsaken God and broken His covenant many times, the Almighty gave to Jeremiah the promise we have read in our passage today. But there is something missing here. When the first covenant with Abraham was inaugurated, it was sealed by blood (Gen. 15:9-10). Such was the case also when the covenant was renewed at Sinai (Exod. 24:8). However, there is no mention of blood in Jeremiah's covenant. It is like a legal document which has been drawn up, but not signed or witnessed. When and how was it made valid? I think you will already know how that validation came, but we must wait until tomorrow to have the full legal details.

FURTHER STUDY

Gen. 21:22-34; 31:43-55

1. What were the terms of the covenant between Abraham and Abimelech?

2. What were the terms between Laban and Jacob?

O Father, I am impressed as I follow the track of Your purposes through the flow of history. I see that nothing was left to chance. You planned my salvation down to the tiniest detail. Thank You, dear Father. In Jesus' name. Amen.

A great moment in history

FOR READING & MEDITATION – HEBREWS 13:5-21

'... the God of peace ... through the blood of the eternal covenant
brought back from the dead our Lord ...' (v.20)

We ended yesterday by looking at God's promise of a new covenant as given to the prophet Jeremiah – a covenant, we noted, which had no ratifying blood. We described it, you will remember, as being like a legal document awaiting a signature. We have to pass on a further six centuries to learn how that covenant was ratified when, after years of patient waiting and increasing expectancy, the Son of God stood in an upper room in Jerusalem and announced that the ratifying blood of God's new covenant would be none other than His own. Is it possible to exaggerate the staggering nature of that moment?

FURTHER STUDY

1 Sam. 18:1-4;
20:1-17;
2 Sam. 9:1-10

1. Why did Jonathan make a covenant with David?

2. How did David fulfil the covenant?

Picture the scene with me once again. Jesus takes up the bread which was normally used at this stage in the Passover service and dedicates it to a new purpose. The ancient Passover, celebrated in the same way for centuries, is now being given a new direction. Luke says, 'In the same way ... he took the cup, saying, "This cup is the new covenant in my blood, which is poured out for you"' (Luke 22:20).

It was at this point that the Passover was transformed so that it became the Lord's Supper of the new covenant. Jesus was saying, in effect, 'The new covenant promised by Jeremiah has been waiting for centuries to be ratified and sealed. Now that hour has come, and the blood of sealing is the blood that will flow out of My own veins. This cup is the symbol of that. Drink it in remembrance of Me.' So every time you approach the Communion table, let your mind focus on the thrilling thought that Jesus died to bring us into a new covenant relationship with God.

O God my Father, when I see what initiating this new covenant meant for You and Your Son, I feel like bowing to worship You. You put everything You had into my redemption; help me put everything I have into making it known. In Jesus' name. Amen.

FOR READING & MEDITATION - HEBREWS 8:1-13

'... the covenant of which he is mediator is superior to the old one,
and is founded on better promises.' (v.6)

Now that we have seen a little of what the covenant
Jesus referred to is all about, we must spend some more
time meditating on the implications of it. It is described as
a 'new' covenant to distinguish it from the old covenant
which was mediated mostly through obedience to law.

This is why some Christians refer to the Old Testament
covenant as the covenant of law and the new covenant,
announced through Jeremiah and ratified with Christ's
blood, as the covenant of grace. The difference between
the covenant of law and the covenant of grace is this: the
law said, 'Do this and you shall live'; grace says,
'I will do it for you.' This is why the new covenant
supersedes the old – Christ lives within us to
provide the power to reach the standards God
requires of us.

**FURTHER
STUDY**

Heb. 9:1-28

1. What does the
law require?

Another thing to be observed as we look at the
nature of this new covenant is that it is utterly
and entirely an undertaking of God. Normally, as
we said, a covenant involves two parties, and the
principle underlying it is this: if you will do your
part, I will do mine. But the word *diatheke* suggests that
it is a covenant ordained and laid down by an authority.
It is not God and man making an equal contribution, but
God taking on the full obligation. There is a human side to
it, of course, but compared to God's input, it is as if it is
all of Him. There need be no fear that because of human
weakness and frailty it will break down, for, as one quaint
preacher put it, 'God thought it, Christ bought it, the Holy
Spirit wrought it, and though the devil fought it – thank
God, I've got it.' And, may I add – got it for ever!

2. Why is the
new covenant
better?

**O Father, the more I contemplate the wonder of Your covenant
love, the more I want to bow my knees in gratitude. But I know
You want more than my gratitude - You want my obedience also.
For it is obedience that opens the door to Your power. Amen.**

Forgiven!

FOR READING & MEDITATION - EPHESIANS 1:3-14

'In him we have redemption through his blood, the forgiveness
of sins ...' (v.7)

We have touched on the fact that one of the exciting features of the new covenant was that it promised the remission of sins, but let us now bring that aspect into closer focus. Under the old covenant, sin could not be dealt with effectively: '... it is impossible for the blood of bulls and goats to take away sins' (Heb. 10:4). The Old Testament sacrifices served as a type or shadow, which meant that God did not overlook sin, but rather 'looked over' it to the coming sacrifice of His Son on Calvary.

FURTHER STUDY

Heb. 10:1-22

1. Why is it impossible for the blood of bulls to remove sin?

2. Why is it possible for Christ's blood to remove sin?

I wonder if you are someone who struggles with the use of the word 'blood' in books or hymns about the Christian faith. If so, I would encourage you to look again at the phrase 'the blood of Christ', for it is one of the most sacred and significant phrases in Scripture. Rather than being a morbid phrase, it speaks of forgiveness, cleansing, redemption, life.

Blood flows everywhere in the Bible. The red river runs from Genesis to Revelation: cut the Bible anywhere and it bleeds. For you see, it is not just by the death of Christ that we are saved – it is through death *by the shedding of blood.* His blood is covenant blood. It is not merely blood poured out in affectionate self-giving. It is the blood of a covenant sacrifice in which God commits Himself to us in the most solemn way possible. The well-known hymn puts it beautifully:

His oath, His cov'nant and His blood
Support me in the whelming flood
When all around my soul gives way
He then is all my hope and stay.

Edward Mote (1797–1874)

O my Father, how can You be so gracious to the ungracious, so loving to the unloving, so considerate to the inconsiderate? Your love overwhelms my heart. I freely receive what You so freely bestow. Thank You, Father. Amen.

FOR READING & MEDITATION – PSALM 95:1-11

'Let us come before him with thanksgiving ...' (v.2)

We come now to look at the fourth aspect of Communion – the aspect of celebration. One of the words that is becoming increasingly popular in Christian circles to describe the Lord's Supper is the word 'Eucharist'. It simply means, 'Thanksgiving'.

The Communion service ought not only to be a time in which we remind ourselves that we are a corporate body, meeting together to commemorate the death of our Lord and to remember the nature of the new covenant, but a time when we open up our hearts to God in joyful celebration and praise. Jesus, you will remember, prior to distributing the bread and wine at the Last Supper, 'gave thanks' (Matt. 26:26–27). And following the conclusion of the Passover, we read that He and His disciples sang a hymn (Matt. 26:30). A Communion service (so I believe), though focusing on very solemn and profound truths, ought not to be doleful.

I remember the Communion services I attended in the early days of my Christian experience, and I could never understand why the people in my church were so gloomy and sorrowful. When I questioned them about this they said, 'The sufferings of Christ on the cross ought to be responded to with sympathy and sorrow.' 'That is true,' I used to say. 'We must start there, but surely we must not stop there. After we remember His suffering and sacrifice for us, our hearts should respond in grateful worship and praise.' After many years as a Christian, I have seen no reason to change my thinking. So I say with increased conviction – at the Communion table, we not only remind ourselves of our Lord's redemptive sacrifice, we *rejoice* in it too.

FURTHER STUDY

Psa. 98:1-9;
Psa. 100:1-5

1. Why was the psalmist jubilant?

2. How do we enter God's presence?

O Lord Jesus, You who knew how to give thanks in everything, teach me how to catch this note anew and apply it to every part of my life. For Your own dear name's sake. Amen.

Enjoying Him

FOR READING & MEDITATION - JOHN 6:22-40

'... I am the bread of life. He who comes to me will never
go hungry ...' (v.35)

We continue reflecting on the thought that the Communion service is to be a time of rejoicing and worshipful celebration. E.F. Kevan points out that the Lord's Supper is a meal and throughout time, 'meals have been the occasions of conviviality and of friendship'. He goes on to say, 'A feast is the method of expressing joy. When you have a birthday, you have a birthday party; when you get married, you have a wedding meal. When you want to express gladness in any matter, you have a common meal together, and this is one of the aspects that the Lord has taken up in His ordinance of the Lord's Supper.'

FURTHER STUDY

Psa. 104:1-35

1. Why did God provide bread and wine?

2. What was the psalmist's response?

As we have not yet developed the thought that the Lord's Supper is a spiritual feast, this seems to be an appropriate moment to do so. Our text for today, although not having a direct reference to the Communion, is nevertheless a description of what happens when we meet together at the Lord's table – we *feed* on Him. Just as we *eat* the bread – not merely look at it – and just as we *drink* the wine, and not merely observe it, so in the Communion we partake of Christ and feed our souls on Him.

One critic of the Gospels has described the verse which says, 'Unless you eat the flesh of the Son of Man' as 'Christian cannibalism'. He evidently did not understand how the soul can draw strength and nourishment from regular contact with Christ. It is a mystery, but don't let the mystery of it hinder you from experiencing and enjoying it. I say 'enjoying it', for one can no more partake of Christ without enjoying Him than one can partake of a good meal and not experience a degree of pleasure.

Blessed Lord Jesus, the more I feed on You, the more I enjoy You. And the more I enjoy You, the more I want of You. Only You can truly satisfy. I am eternally grateful. Amen.

The Vision

One day Jesus *will* return. One day we will join with countless others in giving God the glory He is due. One day all that is wrong will be put right.

In the next issue, join us as we embark on a devotional journey through the book of Revelation to discover truths that will strengthen our faith and our mission. Topics considered include:

- The supremacy of Christ
- Our part in sharing Jesus
- Hope for those who are faithful

Allow the apostle John's vision of our wonderful Saviour to become yours too.

Also available as ebook/esubscription

Let's celebrate!

FOR READING & MEDITATION - 1 CORINTHIANS 5:6-11
'... Christ, our Passover lamb, has been sacrificed.
Therefore let us keep the Festival ...' (vv.7-8)

In the verses before us today, Paul expresses the common sense of joy and exhilaration that we experience in Christ by alluding to the best known of all the Jewish feasts – the feast of Passover. We have said so much about the Passover in these meditations that there seems little else left to say, but actually there is. Although, strictly speaking, the Passover was the communal meal eaten during the evening of what the Jews call 'the fifteenth Nisan', it came to be applied also to the week-long Feast of Unleavened Bread which followed.

FURTHER STUDY

Neh. 8:9-12;
Phil. 4:1-7

1. How do we gain strength?

2. How can we always be rejoicing?

Both the Passover meal itself and the week that followed was, and is to this day, a time of great rejoicing for the nation of Israel. The basis of that rejoicing was their deliverance from the tyranny and bondage of Egypt. However, a greater exodus than that enjoyed by Israel has been effected in human history. It is the deliverance wrought by Jesus Christ on the cross of Calvary. Because He, the Paschal Lamb, has been slain and because by His blood we have been set free, we are exhorted to keep the feast.

What can Paul be meaning here? Is he saying that we ought to keep the ancient feast of the Passover just as the Jews do to this day? No, he is saying that the whole of the Christian life should be conceived of as a festival in which we continuously celebrate what God has done for us in Christ. But although the Christian life is a continuous festival, the Lord's Supper – the particular Christian equivalent to the Passover – is a powerful means of crystallising truth and bringing home to our hearts the need and reason for continuous celebration.

O Father, when I see how much joy ought to be pulsing through my life, forgive me that I do not always take hold of it. Your cup is upturned to give, help me to turn up my cup to receive. For Jesus' sake I ask it. Amen.

Sinners saved by grace

FOR READING & MEDITATION - REVELATION 5:1-14

'Worthy is the Lamb ... to receive power and wealth and wisdom and strength and honour and glory and praise!' (v.12)

Although, as we said yesterday, the Christian life is in many ways an unending festival, the Communion helps us (as did the Passover for the Israelites) to keep in focus the reason that lies behind our rejoicing – namely, the sacrificial death of our Lord Jesus Christ, God's Paschal Lamb. The Lord's Supper, as we said, is the Christian equivalent of the Passover and just as the Passover was central to Israel's life and identity, so the Lord's Supper is central to the Church's life of celebration.

There are many reasons that lie behind the praise of God's people when they meet together, but the central reason is always to be gratitude for our deliverance from the bondage of sin as accomplished through our Saviour's atoning death on the cross. When we focus on the cross, we are caught up in the worship of heaven and join with the angels and archangels to acknowledge the worth of our Creator and our Redeemer. To focus on the cross and not want to burst forth in praise means that we do not really understand what it is all about.

We attend church for many reasons – to find answers to life's perplexing questions, to find comfort when times are hard, to offer encouragement to others, and these are all valid occupations. However, the foremost purpose for our meeting together is to offer God praise for His great salvation. Everything else flows out of this. Christians sometimes make the rafters ring with their praise. And why not? If angels sing of the cross and have never tasted of its power, then how much more we, who are sinners saved by grace?

FURTHER STUDY

Heb. 13:11-15; Rev. 7:9-17

1. What is our offering to God?

2. Describe the atmosphere of heaven?

O Lord Jesus, when I realise how Your nail-pierced hand has passed over my life and cleansed me from every sin, my feelings will just not go into words. Just saying 'Thank You' seems so very inadequate. Yet I mean it. Thank You. Amen.

'Table fellowship'

FOR READING & MEDITATION – OBADIAH vv.6-15
'... those who eat your bread will set a trap for you ...' (v.7)

We come now to the last of our five aspects of the Communion – the aspect of commitment. In ancient times, and in some parts of the world today, sitting and eating a meal at someone's table implied a certain degree of commitment. You may have heard the phrase, 'the salt of the covenant', which arises from eating salt with someone, or in other words, having a meal with them. It was expected of those who ate at someone's table that they would never do anything to violate the friendship that had been shown them.

FURTHER STUDY

Lev. 2:11-13;
Josh. 9:1-20

1. Why would God ban yeast and honey but approve salt?

2. How did the Israelites honour a tricky covenant?

This kind of 'table fellowship' is illustrated in the passage before us today, where we see that the sacred loyalties which had been worked out together were being violated. Note the words again: '... those who eat your bread will set a trap for you ...' Another verse that points out the sacredness of table fellowship is Psalm 41:9: 'Even my close friend, whom I trusted, he who shared my bread, has lifted up his heel against me.'

The thing that troubled the psalmist was not so much that he had been wronged, but that he had been wronged by someone who had sat at his own table. It was this verse, you remember, which Jesus used in John 13:18 with reference to Judas. It is clear from Scripture that taking a meal with someone implies a trust and a pledge. It is not dissimilar to the table of Communion. Jesus expects that when we eat and drink at His table, we will not be party to anything that would injure His cause or violate His eternal principles. Dare we eat and drink with Him and then go out and bring dishonour to His name?

O Lord Jesus, I tremble inwardly when I realise just what is involved in coming to Your table. I don't want ever to let You down. Empower me so that I will be a faithful follower of You – all the days of my life. In Your dear name I pray. Amen.

Self-examination

FOR READING & MEDITATION - 1 CORINTHIANS 10:14-22

'... you cannot have a part in both the Lord's table and the table of demons.' (v.21)

We saw yesterday the importance of 'table fellowship' – the principle that once you 'eat salt' with someone, there is an implied commitment that you will never violate the friendship. All this takes on a deeper significance when we remember God's warnings to His people not to partake in heathen feasts (see Exod. 34:15; Num. 25:2-3).

A similar point is made in the passage before us today in the context of the Lord's Supper: 'Consider the people of Israel: Do not those who eat the sacrifices participate in the altar?' (v.18). Paul is saying here that for an Israelite to eat of a heathen sacrifice was to associate himself with all that the altar signifies. In verse 20 he goes on to say, '... the sacrifices of pagans are offered to demons, not to God, and I do not want you to be participants with demons.'

The clear meaning of all this is that the table at which we eat is, whether we realise it or not, the place where our loyalty is pledged. We cannot eat of the Lord's table if we are at the same time eating at the table of demons. This is why we should always approach the Lord's table with a willingness to bring our habits, our motives and our lifestyle under careful scrutiny, and be prepared to break with all those things that are dishonouring to Jesus.

Note also that self-examination should end in an act of commitment: 'A man ought to examine himself before he eats of the bread and drinks of the cup' (1 Cor. 11:28). The purpose of self-examination is not to beat ourselves over the head with a spiritual club and say, 'I am a terrible Christian', but to surrender our failures to Christ, receive His forgiveness and move a little closer towards Him.

FURTHER STUDY

Psa. 139:23-24;
2 Cor. 13:5-7

1. What was the cry of the psalmist?

2. What exam should Christians take regularly?

Loving Father, I am challenged – but I know that *Your* challenges lead to life. Reveal in me any hidden resentment or wrong attitudes, and help me to let go of these things. Forgive me and make me clean again. In Jesus' name. Amen.

A spiritual health check

FOR READING & MEDITATION - 1 PETER 4:12-19

'For it is time for judgment to begin with the family of God ...' (v.17)

Today we hit a solemn and serious note – but one we cannot and should not avoid. If we fail to examine ourselves when we come to the Communion table and surrender to the Lord those things that are wrong, then they will become the virus within us that will bring about spiritual ill-health.

The apostle Paul told the Corinthians, 'Whoever eats the bread or drinks the cup of the Lord in an unworthy manner will be guilty of sinning against the body and blood of the Lord' (1 Cor. 11:27). What did he mean? Eating and drinking unworthily suggests participating in the Communion in a factious, unloving, critical and judgmental spirit. This is a sin, not just against the Body of Christ, the Church, but against the Person of Christ as symbolised in the elements.

FURTHER STUDY

Matt. 7:1-5;
2 Cor. 6:16-7:1;
Heb. 12:14-29

1. What should we avoid?

2. What should we embrace?

Almost every local church has those in its midst who come to the Lord's table bent on examination – not of themselves, but of others. I have no hesitation in saying that this attitude produces spiritual disharmony. There were some in the Corinthian church who, because they failed to examine themselves at the Lord's table and thus maintained wrong attitudes and wrong motives, became weak and sickly – some even died.

You see, spiritual ill-health can soon turn to physical ill-health – even death. Dare I say it? I must – there are some in the Christian Church who are sicker than they should be, for they allow the virus of wrong attitudes to take root in their souls. If we approach the Lord's table in the right spirit, then we will be able to approach the whole of life in the right spirit – period.

O Father, I am so quick to find fault with others, but You call me to pay attention to the state of my own spiritual health. Again I ask that You would cleanse me and make me whole. In the name of Jesus. Amen.

FOR READING & MEDITATION - 1 SAMUEL 15:10-26
'To obey is better than sacrifice ...' (v.22)

As we begin to draw our meditations to a close, we return to the sentiment I expressed at the beginning of this issue – that one of the greatest needs of the contemporary Christian Church is to return meaning to the Communion. In view of this, we need to ask ourselves a personal and searching question: have we allowed our familiarity with the act of 'Holy Communion' to breed within us a sense of complacency? I would argue that to a large extent we have.

Roy Peacock, in his book, *This Do Ye*, says, 'To many, the Communion service has taken the form of an abstract set of actions performed, as one would watch a stage play, with interested or perhaps uninterested detachment. No longer do we hear the voice of Jesus, saying, "Do this in remembrance of me". No more is there the revelation that amazes us, challenges us and changes us, for our ears have waxed heavy and our eyes have been shut by a complacency of satisfaction.' He is generalising, of course, but even if the charge of complacency does not apply to us, every one of us cannot help but benefit from the attempt to comprehend more deeply the meaning of the Communion.

FURTHER STUDY

Num. 9:1-5;
1 Cor. 11:23-26

1. What did the Lord command?

2. What did Jesus command?

We meet around many tables during the course of our lives, but no table is more significant and meaningful than the one on which we place the simple emblems of bread and wine and celebrate Jesus' vicarious death and victorious resurrection. And remember: the Communion service is not a matter of inclination – it is a matter of command. Jesus said, 'Do this in remembrance of me.' As we said earlier – Jesus' sacrifice is of too great importance not to be regularly brought to mind and celebrated.

O God my Father, help me to embrace the meaning of Your Communion service. Help me never to lose the sense of its significance. In Jesus' name I pray. Amen.

'Until He comes'

FOR READING & MEDITATION - REVELATION 22:7-21
'Behold, I am coming soon!' (v.7)

We remind ourselves, on this our last day together, of what we described earlier as 'the five c's of Communion' – community, commemoration, covenant, celebration and commitment. Most Christians, irrespective of denomination, will agree that whenever we approach the Lord's table, we must recognise that it is a corporate act in which we focus our attention on Christ's redemptive death on Calvary, remind ourselves of its covenant nature, rejoice in the great benefits of the atonement and pledge our loyalty to Him who loved us and gave Himself for us.

FURTHER STUDY

Rev. 19:6-9; 21:1-7; 22:1-6

1. How will Communion be consummated?

2. Describe our heavenly hope.

There is just one more word I have to say before we close – the Lord's Supper is a wonderful but only a temporary provision for the Christian Church. We shall not celebrate it in eternity, for there faith will be lost in sight – we do it only 'until He comes'. As we move away from the holy table, we carry with us the thrilling thought that just as Jesus came at His first advent, so will He come again at His second advent.

The Lord's Supper commands, therefore, a confident belief in Jesus' second coming; it is the token of our Master's return. Indeed, without that belief it cannot be said to be truly celebrated. So permit me to repeat it once again – the Lord's Supper is 'until He comes'. This compelling verse puts it still more powerfully:

And thus that dark betrayal night
With the last advent we unite
By one blest chain of loving rite
Until He come.

George Rawson (1807–1889)

O Father, what can I say? My heart cries out in eager anticipation, 'Come, Lord Jesus.' Amen.

4 EASY WAYS TO ORDER:

1. Phone in your credit card order: **01252 784710** (Mon-Fri, 9.30am - 5pm)

2. Visit our Online Store at **www.cwr.org.uk/store**

3. Send this form together with your payment to:
   CWR, Waverley Abbey House, Waverley Lane, Farnham, Surrey GU9 8EP

4. Visit your local Christian bookshop

For a list of our National Distributors, who supply countries outside the UK, visit www.cwr.org.uk/distributors

YOUR DETAILS (REQUIRED FOR ORDERS AND DONATIONS)

Name:	**CWR ID No.** (if known):
Home Address:	
	Postcode:
Telephone No. (for queries):	**Email:**

PUBLICATIONS

TITLE	QTY	PRICE	TOTAL
		Total publications	

All CWR adult Bible-reading notes are also available in ebook and email subscription format.
Visit www.cwr.org.uk for further information.

UK p&p: up to £24.99 = **£2.99**; £25.00 and over = **FREE**	
Elsewhere p&p: up to £10 = **£4.95**; £10.01 - £50 = **£6.95**; £50.01 - £99.99 = **£10**; £100 and over = **£30**	
Please allow 14 days for delivery **Total publications and p&p A**	

SUBSCRIPTIONS* (NON DIRECT DEBIT)

	QTY	PRICE (INCLUDING P&P)			TOTAL
		UK	Europe	Elsewhere	
Every Day with Jesus (1yr, 6 issues)		£15.95	£19.95	Please contact nearest National Distributor or CWR direct	
Large Print *Every Day with Jesus* (1yr, 6 issues)		£15.95	£19.95		
Inspiring Women Every Day (1yr, 6 issues)		£15.95	£19.95		
Life Every Day (Jeff Lucas) (1yr, 6 issues)		£15.95	£19.95		
Cover to Cover Every Day (1yr, 6 issues)		£15.95	£19.95		
Mettle: 14-18s (1yr, 3 issues)		£14.50	£16.60		
YP's: 11-15s (1yr, 6 issues)		£15.95	£19.95		
Topz: 7-11s (1yr, 6 issues)		£15.95	£19.95		
Total Subscriptions (Subscription prices already include postage and packing) **B**					

Please circle which bimonthly issue you would like your subscription to commence from:
Jan/Feb Mar/Apr May/Jun Jul/Aug Sep/Oct Nov/Dec

* Only use this section for subscriptions paid for by credit/debit card or
cheque. For Direct Debit subscriptions see overleaf.

CONTINUED OVERLEAF >>

PAYMENT DETAILS

☐ I enclose a cheque/PO made payable to CWR for the amount of: £ _____

☐ Please charge my credit/debit card.

Cardholder's name (in BLOCK CAPITALS) _____

Card No. ☐☐☐☐ ☐☐☐☐ ☐☐☐☐ ☐☐☐☐

Expires end ☐☐☐☐   Security Code ☐☐☐

GIFT TO CWR   ☐ Please send me an acknowledgement of my gift   **C** ☐

GIFT AID (YOUR HOME ADDRESS REQUIRED, SEE OVERLEAF)

giftaid it

I am a UK taxpayer and want CWR to reclaim the tax on all my donations for the four years prior to this year **and on** all donations I make from the date of this Gift Aid declaration until further notice.*

Taxpayer's Full Name (in BLOCK CAPITALS) _____

Signature _____ **Date** _____

*I understand I must pay an amount of Income/Capital Gains Tax at least equal to the tax the charity reclaims in the tax year.

GRAND TOTAL (Total of A, B, & C) ☐

SUBSCRIPTIONS BY DIRECT DEBIT (UK BANK ACCOUNT HOLDERS ONLY)

Subscriptions cost £15.95 (except *Mettle*: £14.50) for one year for delivery within the UK. Please tick relevant boxes and fill in the form be

☐ *Every Day with Jesus* (1yr, 6 issues)
☐ Large Print *Every Day with Jesus* (1yr, 6 issues)
☐ *Inspiring Women Every Day* (1yr, 6 issues)
☐ *Life Every Day* (Jeff Lucas) (1yr, 6 issues)

☐ *Cover to Cover Every Day* (1yr, 6 issues)
☐ *Mettle*: 14-18s (1yr, 3 issues)
☐ *YP's*: 11-15s (1yr, 6 issues)
☐ *Topz*: 7-11s (1yr, 6 issues)

Issue to commence fro
☐ Jan/Feb ☐ Jul/Aug
☐ Mar/Apr ☐ Sep/Oct
☐ May/Jun ☐ Nov/Dec

CWR   Instruction to your Bank or Building Society to pay by Direct Debit   **DIRECT Debit**

Please fill in the form and send to: CWR, Waverley Abbey House, Waverley Lane, Farnham, Surrey GU9 8EP

Name and full postal address of your Bank or Building Society

To: The Manager _____ Bank/Building Society
Address _____
_____ Postcode _____

Name(s) of Account Holder(s) _____

Branch Sort Code ☐☐ ☐☐ ☐☐

Bank/Building Society account number ☐☐☐☐☐☐☐☐

Originator's Identification Number: 4 2 0 4 8 7

Reference: ☐☐☐☐☐☐☐☐☐☐☐☐☐☐☐☐☐☐

Instruction to your Bank or Building Society

Please pay CWR Direct Debits from the account detailed in this Instruction subj to the safeguards assured by the Direct Debit Guarantee.
I understand that this Instruction may remain with CWR and, if so, details will be passed electronically to my Bank/Building Society.

Signature(s) _____

Date _____

Banks and Building Societies may not accept Direct Debit Instructions for some types of account